# DAY OF GLORY
## The Guns at Lexington and Concord

by Philip Spencer

*Interior illustrations by Peter Burchard*

AN
**APPLE**
PAPERBACK

SCHOLASTIC INC.
New York Toronto London Auckland Sydney

ISBN 0-590-44415-8

Copyright © 1955 by Philip Spencer.
All rights reserved. Published by Scholastic Inc.
APPLE PAPERBACKS is a registered trademark of Scholastic Inc.

12 11 10 9 8 7 6 5 4 3 2                    3 4 5 6/9

Printed in the U.S.A.                              40

# CONTENTS

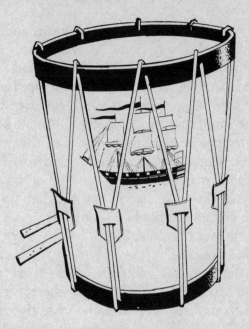

## DAY OF GLORY: *Seven P.M.*

*T*he town gate of Boston was by now, far behind. At the next winding of the road, the last Cambridge house would appear. Then it would be little but farmlands ahead—and Lexington.

Already Solomon Brown noticed the difference in the air. With every step of the horse, it seemed the fragrance of April was growing richer and clearer: grass, earth, leaves and blossoms. The strong smell of ocean, that had drawn the boy on toward Boston in the morning, was gone. For

1

once he was glad to be rid of the town, and very glad to be on his way home to Lexington.

Last night, at supper, his father had said: "We'll be needing a shovel to make up for the one that's broken, Solomon; and for six weeks I've been promising your mother a new kettle. Tomorrow should be a mild day. Get the wagon ready. You'll take eggs and butter and two boxes of chickens to market."

"Are you sure we should let the lad go this time?" Solomon's mother had asked.

"And why not this time, Sarah?"

"Boston's not safe."

Even the younger children knew what their mother meant. For years, everywhere in the colonies, there had been trouble with the rulers overseas. The King and Parliament seemed determined to remind the Americans that they were not a free people.

Their money, their ways of making a living, their very lives were to be controlled by the rulers across the ocean. They were ordered to do business with no other country than England. Their houses were searched without warrants to put a stop to the West Indies trade by which many of them lived.

Restriction was added to restriction, tax to tax. Everywhere, the Americans had resisted these attempts to have strangers rule their affairs. In every colony, patriots had banded together for liberty, with Boston the center of resistance.

The King had sent his own men over to collect the taxes and to see that his orders were carried out. The people of Boston had become so angry that, soon, he had to ship soldiers across the sea to protect his tax collectors. The troops did a lot of mischief in the city. When the citizens objected to their behavior, the soldiers fired into an unarmed crowd, killing and wounding many.

The leaders of the people, especially Samuel Adams, John Hancock and Joseph Warren, sent the news of this "Boston Massacre" far and wide. After the Massacre, the troops had been withdrawn from the city itself. Now they were back again, in greater force, bolder and more troublesome than before.

It was the "Tea Party" that had brought the soldiers back, that had made the English declare "the town of Boston ought to be knocked about their ears and destroyed."

A tax had been put upon tea brought into the colonies. In Boston, Samuel Adams warned the ships not to land the cargo; but the warning was disregarded. Patriots, calling themselves "Sons of Liberty," dumped the boxes of tea into the waters of the harbor.

For this act, the King took a terrible revenge.

Since Boston would have no tea, he declared it should have no trade at all. Its port was closed, its government put in the hands of the military.

Throughout the winter months the people had a hard time, without work or food. Still they refused to pay for the tea, and from the surrounding villages and the distant colonies they received gifts and messages of support. When the King saw that the people would not give in, even when they were starved, he decided to arrest their leaders and to crush the whole city by sending more troops.

Now that the cold weather was over, the soldiers were impatient to get out into the streets and countryside and show what they could do. Mr. Brown knew this—but he also knew that his son was strong and brave, and clever enough to take care of himself.

"Solomon is a man, Sarah. In two or three years he'll be thinking of a wife and farm of his own. How long can you be worrying about him as though he were still a child?"

His wife sighed. "There's no telling what the soldiers will be up to next. How long is it since they tarred and feathered that man from Billerica? Hardly a month! Wouldn't they think it great sport to overturn Solomon's wagon or unharness the horse?"

"Don't worry about me, Mother," Solomon an-

swered. "Father's right. It's time you thought of
me as a grown man. If Captain Parker let me be
a Minute Man and drill with the others, you can
bet I'll be all right in Boston, too. I promise, this
once, to stay out of the redcoats' way."

That was last night. At noon, today, he'd gone
through Boston's town gate as sure of himself as
ever. The same sentries were there as had let
him go by two months ago. They knew him and
his wagon—even nodded as he drove by.

But once inside the city, he felt he'd never
been there before. True, the street signs were the
same—the buildings had not changed their shape
or color. But most of the shutters were tightly
closed, right in the middle of the day! And the
lips of the people seemed to be closed just as
tightly. The wonderful roar of a great, healthy
port had disappeared. In its place Solomon could
hear, wherever he went, the tread of British soldiers.

From the top of a hill he looked down at the
harbor. How different it was from the harbor he
used to see! A year ago, hundreds of beautiful
trading vessels were there, with sails of every
color. They had stretched from the wharves to the
far-off horizon—like a magic carpet—so crowded
that in places the water could not be seen.

Today, not a single one of these ships remained.
It was as though an evil wind had swept them

off the face of the earth. Only the gunboats of
the British lay in the harbor now—and towering
above the others with its many cannon, the man-
of-war, *Somerset*.

Solomon drove the wagon down to the market
place. But he sold only one box of chickens. The
other he kept hidden in the wagon, as his father
had instructed him to do. After buying the shovel
and kettle, he set out for Faneuil Hall, where last
year he had come to hear great patriots speak.

Now, very few of the resistance leaders were
still in Boston. Since the King had ordered them
to be arrested, they were hiding in other towns.
The two whom the King particularly hated, Samuel Adams and John Hancock, were this minute
at a house not far from Solomon's farm, in Lexington.

The Assembly Hall was upstairs; but the first
floor was used as a butcher shop. Solomon went
in by the back door and waited until the few
customers had left.

"Can I help you, young man?"

"I'd like to see Mr. Rogers."

The clerk looked at Solomon's covered box.
"Right through that door," he said, quietly.

Rogers was on a ladder, busily marking and
counting packages on the shelves. He didn't hear
Solomon come in.

"Excuse me, sir."

The old man was so startled he almost lost his balance on the ladder. However, when Solomon told him that the chickens were a gift to the poor of Boston, Rogers smiled warmly and stepped down.

"Where are you from?"

"Lexington."

"Ah! And how," he whispered, with a wink, "are your guests today?"

Solomon knew he must be asking about Adams and Hancock, so he winked back and nodded. But he also knew that their whereabouts were supposed to be kept secret, and that he must say not one word about them.

For a moment, the old man seemed undecided about something. He looked away with a frown. Then he made up his mind, and turned to the boy. "Wait! Take these." He handed him a packet. "Make sure it reaches *no one* but Adams and Hancock. A few of the papers are secret. If you'd rather not take the chance, I'll try to get it into Lexington some other way."

"Of course I'll take it, sir. It's an honor."

With redcoats everywhere, the boy decided not to spend any more time in the city. It was uncomfortable—almost frightening. He wanted to get back to Lexington before dark.

As he neared the town gate he noticed that, since noon, the number of sentries had been doubled and that all who wanted to go past were now being stopped. He feared they might search him and find the secret papers. But just as one of the guards was about to stop the horse, another interrupted.

"Don't waste your time. Let the lad through. I know him. He's only a country bumpkin."

Even after he had left the town gate far behind, Solomon continued to worry. What was the meaning of the doubled guard? Was Governor Gage closing the city?

He whipped the horse so that it flew around the curves in the road. Just ahead, between him and the sunset, loomed nine British officers on horseback. Never before had he seen or heard of so many outside the city at once. And so late in the day, and all going together, away from Boston!

His first thought was to wheel around, but some of the officers had turned at the sound of his approach. If he tried to escape, they might all set out after him.

They rode very slowly, and he kept getting closer. Once or twice they looked back at him, and then they would nod to one another, whispering and pointing in various directions. It seemed they were just as nervous about Solomon as he was about them, and were trying to act as

though there was nothing unusual about their
presence on the Lexington road.

Now he was nearly up to them. They gave him
room to pass. His heart drummed wildly and his
face burned. "Good evening!" he blurted out,
trying to sound calm.

"Good evening!" one of the officers echoed.

Just then the wind, which had been growing
stronger since the sunset, blew aside their greatcoats, and Solomon caught a glimpse of something which the coats had hidden. He recognized
the icy glitter of pistols.

Now, he surely had news to tell at home—not
to his parents first, or his cousin Francis. What he
had seen concerned all of Lexington—perhaps
even all of the thirteen colonies! Captain Parker
must be warned, then the "guests" at Reverend
Clark's house.

Pistols were on the way, hidden under British
greatcoats, and the leaders of the people were in
danger. Solomon cracked the whip, and disappeared into the dusk.

## DAY OF GLORY: *Eight P. M.*

*T*he parlor of Dr. Warren's house, in Boston, was filled with visitors. A Negro servant looked in from the kitchen. Noticing that the room had become quite dark, he lit the lamps and locked the shutters.

There was a knocking, and the conversation stopped. All eyes turned to the door, as Boston John hurried to open it.

It was old Rogers, stopping by on his way home from the Faneuil Hall butcher shop.

"Come in, Rogers, and help us wait!"

From the hallway the butcher looked slowly around the parlor, nodding to those he knew, searching for the one face that was missing.

The other visitors remained silent, as he joined their circle. Nowadays, every word must be carefully chosen—even in front of old friends. Too many secrets were reaching the ears of the enemy. They waited, knowing that Rogers would ask again what each in turn had already asked.

"Where's the doctor?"

A gray-bearded man shrugged. "Nobody knows. He told *me* to be here at 7:30 sharp."

"I've been waiting since 7:20," another said. "It's nearly eight o'clock now."

Boston John came out of the kitchen again, looking worried. He unlocked the door and peered through the dusk that had settled on Hanover Street. Groups of men were walking past—many more than was usual for such an hour. Almost all of them were British soldiers heading for the Common. He shook his head. "It's not like the doctor to keep people waiting—not one bit like him. . . . And the supper cold, stone cold!"

"Where was he going?" Rogers asked.

The servant frowned. "Dr. Warren goes to many places that I don't need to know about, and I never ask him."

"Did he go alone?"

"No. With Dr. Eustis, one of his students."

"Then he must be seeing after the sick."

"Not this late." John started for the door again, as though he'd heard footsteps. Then we went slowly back into the kitchen.

The others spoke of many possibilities. Perhaps he'd gone to visit his children. (Since Mrs. Warren's death, they'd been living with their grandmother.) Or he might have stopped at John Scollay's to visit John's daughter. (Mercy Scollay would make a fine wife, and a perfect mother for the children.) Maybe he'd gone to see his own mother in Roxbury. (But that would mean passing the town gate twice. His face was too well known for such a risk to be taken.)

They spoke of many possibilities—but not of the one thing they all dreaded: that their leader had been ambushed by the enemy on his way home.

"What a man he is!" old Rogers said. "I won't forget that Massacre Day speech of his as long as I live. Not the speech itself so much—though it was a beauty—but just his being there, after all the rumors and threats. To have a hundred of them, armed to the teeth, sitting so close that their bayonets could almost touch him! And he looked straight into their faces and called the King a tyrant."

"Did you see what happened when one of the

nearest soldiers held out a handful of bullets to frighten him?" asked a young patriot.

"I saw him look down for a moment once, but he never stopped speaking."

"Yes, he looked down at the bullets, kept on speaking, and dropped his handkerchief over the soldier's hand."

All at once, the hour struck. It shook the room like thunder. What had happened a month before, suddenly seemed far away and small. Tonight might mean an end to speeches, and the beginning of something quite different.

While the hour of eight was striking, two men walked swiftly through the darkening streets of Boston, each with his own thoughts.

The younger one mused: "I'm nothing but a student doctor . . . just starting out. I've done little good or bad. Nobody knows or gives a fig about William Eustis. But tonight I'm taking the most dangerous walk in Boston. How so? Because the man I'm with is Joseph Warren.

"At any corner we may be ambushed by the British, arrested, or shot at. Haven't I myself heard them promise him the gallows? If he's arrested, they'll have plenty of questions for me, too. If he's shot at in the dark, who knows where the bullets might land?

"Yes, I'm frightened. The words are choked

up in my throat, and my legs are ready to cave in. But I keep up with him. It's not easy; his legs are too long and strong, his mind too quick and daring. Yet I keep up. Why?

"Because, out of the corner of my eye, I watch his face that has no hint of fear—his face known to all, his name high on the King's list of traitors. When I see how gladly he marches to each new hour, each new danger, I become ashamed of my buckling legs, and promise that as long as he walks through these streets he'll not walk alone!"

The older one thought: "Eight! three quarters of an hour late, and still a mile from home! Where did the day vanish to? So little done, so much to be done!

"And the children—how could I have promised to stop by to see them tonight? The little ones won't mind. But Joseph—I'm not so sure: (Did I forget, when I was seven?) Elizabeth's still awake, that's certain.

"How deep and grown-up she's suddenly become! And how much of her mother's beauty she shows!

"I should have explained to Elizabeth before this—about the work of the Committees, about the meeting in Philadelphia next month. I should have told her about my own duties here in town. I believe she would understand—most of it anyway; and she'd know how to keep it to herself."

Noticing that his companion was out of breath, Warren slowed down a bit. "Forgive me, Will, I had no idea we were walking so fast. What a fine evening this is! We really should be going as slowly as possible, to enjoy the sky and the breeze. But many friends are waiting in my parlor. Tonight of all nights I had no business being late."

"Can I say something before the others take hold of you?"

The doctor stopped in his tracks. "You can say anything you please, William—except that I should leave Boston tonight."

"That's just what I do want to say. Has your life suddenly become cheap? Boston is a death-trap. Can't you understand? How can you dream of staying on and escaping arrest, while you urge others to fly for their lives?"

"No, my life's not cheap; it's dearer to me than it has ever been in all my thirty-four years. If they take me, it'll be too bad. Meanwhile, I'm free and make the most of it. There's one more thing left for me to do in Boston. When it's done, I'll fly—not to save my skin, but to find a more useful place."

For a moment Joseph Warren gazed thought-fully down at the beloved streets. Then he smiled. "Pretty soon, Will, you can have my patients all to yourself."

"It's not your patients I want, but your safety."

"Safety? Have I, of all people, the right to look for safety? Day after day, I've beaten the drums for freedom—called the young men of Massachusetts away from their fireplaces—told them there *is* no safety while a tyrant oppresses us. Words! What do words mean unless I make them real with my own hands, my own blood?"

Eustis shook his head. "What good would it do for you to be captured or killed?"

They reached the house. By now, more than a dozen Sons of Liberty were awaiting impatiently for their young leader.

At the sight of him they sighed in relief. The talk was now of one thing only! Hundreds of redcoats, foot soldiers and horse, were assembling at the bottom of the Common.

Without a word, the doctor listened to each report; sometimes nodding, occasionally writing down a few words. Only the blaze in his eyes revealed how excited he had become.

When the reports were all finished, it was Warren's turn. One after the other was given instructions: where to go, whom to seek out, when to return. Each nodded and rushed off to his task.

Only now—with William Eustis and one other

remaining—did Warren sit down to supper. While he ate, he explained the plan.

"We know the British are setting out tonight and we're pretty sure of what they want: Adams and Hancock in Lexington; and the guns and powder stored in Concord. All that's left for us to know is whether they'll march across the Neck or ferry across the river into Cambridge. As soon as we're certain, we'll send a signal to our friends, and they'll get the messengers started."

How and by whom and to whom the signal would be sent, he was not at liberty to tell—and they did not ask. Only one thing concerned them now: what part each was to play.

He turned to the remaining Son of Liberty. "There's a young cordwainer a few streets away from here: Billy Dawes. You know the name. Tell him to come at once, ready for his night's work.

"And Will," he added, pointing to Eustis with the drumstick he'd just bitten into, "please find me Paul Revere, *right away!*"

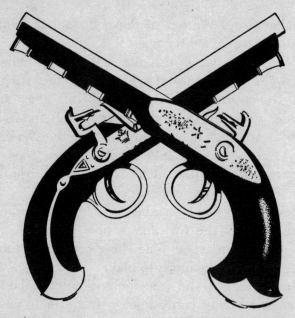

## DAY OF GLORY: *Nine P.M.*

*E*ight men, each carrying a rifle, could be seen by the light from the windows as they marched back and forth in front of the Clark house. They had assembled from all parts of Lexington as soon as Solomon Brown brought the news that British officers were on the road to their village.

Now that night had fallen in earnest, it was becoming quite cold. From time to time, one of the eight would stamp his feet or blow on his fingers for warmth. Another would switch the musket to his left hand so that the right hand could enjoy a pocket. But not a word was said about the sudden cold.

Inside, the supper dishes had long ago been removed. For a while, the talk was of little things —as though to pretend that guards were not really patrolling outside.

"Stir the fire, Jonas! The city folk are shivering!"

At his wife's words, the parson looked around the room. Their guests from Boston had indeed been too polite to say that this country air at night was colder than they could stand. He hurried to the fireplace, and began coaxing the flames back to life. He was happy to do something—just sitting and talking made him sleepy.

Nine o'clock! He and Lucy were usually asleep by now. But of course, there was nothing usual about this evening—with Samuel Adams sitting at their window; with eight muskets moving back and forth outside their door.

All day, his cousin, John Hancock, had been saying how impatient he felt at being cooped up indoors. The Committee of Safety was meeting only a few miles away, yet he'd been ordered not to attend, for fear of his life. Now, however, John lay back dreamily on the sofa which his grandfather had carried into this very house almost fifty years before.

John puffed slowly on his pipe, as Jonas Clark

poked the logs. "Don't bother on my account, cousin. There's enough brewing in the world tonight to keep my blood warm. And as for Miss Dolly (who should be more polite than to read newspapers in company), it would take a greater frost than this to get through all her petticoats."

They turned quickly to the young lady at the table, knowing that, as usual, she would have a ready answer. When those two were married, John Hancock would never lack for lively conversation.

For a moment, she continued staring seriously at a newspaper, as though she hadn't heard. Then, without looking up, she spoke. "Too bad you had to tend the fire, Reverend. I thought there was a man here, ten years younger than you, who could have done it."

"Come now, Miss Dolly," the parson said, "aren't you being a bit hard on your young man? John Hancock isn't likely to have another chance at that old sofa for a long, long time. And tonight, I believe, there isn't a more sensible place for him to be."

"Maybe for *him!* For me, Boston would be far more sensible . . . and interesting. Have you, Mr. Adams, looked into the latest papers out of Boston?"

This was not the first time Dolly had tried to bring Adams into the conversation. He seemed so sad and alone, gazing out of the window. But it was evident that he hadn't even heard her.

What was he thinking about: the guard outside? The news Solomon Brown had brought? The lack of rifles? The steps to be taken at the Congress in Philadelphia? The dangers to be overcome if he and John were to get there? Or was he thinking about Boston, the beloved town for whose liberty he'd given numberless nights and days?

Clark walked over and placed a hand gently on Samuel Adams' shoulder. "The young lady wants to know whether you've looked into the papers Solomon brought home."

Adams shook himself free of his thoughts, and turned with a smile to Dolly. "Forgive me, dear. I didn't hear you. The Boston papers? No . . . I haven't read them yet."

"Then you'll be interested to learn that ten thousand troops are on their way from England to help Gage tame our city."

Adams laughed. "This visit is not news to us. Boston will give them a royal welcome such as the King's troops deserve."

In her mind Dolly contrasted the handsomely outfitted redcoats with the farmers parading outside. "Haven't those children gone home to their mothers yet?" she said, with a laugh. "I think they hope to be heroes before this night is over."

Such words were too much for Hancock. "Let me tell you something about those 'children'. I have known every one of them since the day he was born . . . and the man with my name, who built this house, knew their grandfathers just as well. *You* wouldn't understand, but they happen to be here for a simple reason—simple as they themselves are. They were born in a free village, and can't think of living as slaves."

Hancock's Aunt Lydia had been knitting in a corner listening quietly to the whole conversation. Now she felt the time had come again to smoothe things over.

"I'm surprised, John. Can't you tell, after four years, that the girl is only teasing? Of course she respects the Minute Men of Lexington as much as you do. But, I must admit, the sound of them tramping back and forth, back and forth, gives me the shivers."

Now that her two lady guests had spoken out, Lucy Clark felt she could properly take sides with them. "I also expected them to be on their way home by now. Here it is after nine o'clock, without a sign of trouble. Just because a lad of eighteen saw some British officers on the road, in broad daylight, and *thought* he saw pistols when the wind blew aside their greatcoats, is no reason to keep a whole village in a state of alarm."

Adams put out his arms toward them. "Ladies, ladies—please don't blame *us*. Neither Mr. Hancock nor I think Gage is quite ready to seize us yet. In any case, we're not half as frightened about it as our friends tell us to be. What happens in America from now on will not depend on the safety of one or two men. We've told this to the guard outside, but they insist on protecting us."

"Well spoken, Sam!" Hancock smiled. "A toast to eight brave lads! Cousin Lucy, have you enough flip left to keep our protectors warm— and maybe a few drops for us, too?"

Dolly would not let him have the last word. "Let John fetch it!" she cried. "He's much too spoiled and lazy to be a good husband. Let him serve it, or have none of that wonderful salmon you promised us for tomorrow."

Adams joined in the laughter, then rose and excused himself. "I must get started on my work, before the evening disappears."

They were wishing him good night, when galloping hoofs were heard outside. The guards could be heard ordering a halt. A voice, high-pitched and shrill said, "I must see Mr. Hancock!"

The parson went to the door. "Who is it?"

"A messenger from Menotomy, with an urgent

note to Mr. Hancock from the Committee of Safety."

"Let him in, let him in."

Everyone stood tense, watching Hancock as he read the note. Then, seeing their eagerness, he read it aloud.

"HONORABLE JOHN HANCOCK: I take the liberty of sending you and Samuel Adams a most unusual piece of information just now received.

Having finished our work for the day, around sunset, two of our members left to spend the night in Charlestown. On the way they met a large number of British officers, eight or perhaps nine, approaching on horseback. Our men were greatly alarmed to hear one of the British ask for 'Clark's tavern.' Knowing that this county has no such tavern, and that they must in fact be looking for the Clark house at Lexington, they hastened back to give us the news. Please be advised that your persons are in immediate danger, and act accordingly. We meet tomorrow morning, at nine, and will await word from you. In all haste, ELBRIDGE GERRY, *for the Committee of Safety.*"

A grim silence followed the reading of the letter; then the parson turned to Adams and Hancock. "Wouldn't it be sensible for you to leave this house at once? To spend the night in Woburn?"

"Absolutely not!" Hancock objected. "It hasn't yet reached the point where I'm to run and hide in cellars like a common thief, because nine officers are on a road asking questions."

"And you, Mr. Adams, what do you think?"

"I agree with John. The danger to us should not be exaggerated. As I understand, young Brown and two others are patrolling the road. They can warn us in plenty of time." He bowed to the ladies. "I must get to work. Good night again."

On the way upstairs, Sam Adams listened with a half-smile. The fright had passed. Once more Hancock and his Dolly were playfully throwing insults at each other.

Just as he was closing his door, Adams heard Clark, in a deep but gentle voice, speaking to the guards outside. "The household is not to be disturbed again this evening, except for Solomon Brown or one of the other patrols."

From his worn, little traveling bag Adams took his notebook, and sat down beside the lamp.

Gage

## DAY OF GLORY: *Ten P.M.*

*P*rovince house, which for the past few days had been the busiest spot in Boston, was settling down to sleep.

Now that Lord Percy was gone, Governor Gage summoned one of the servants. "Bolt the doors and shutters. See that the hall lights are out. Then you can retire for the night. I'm expecting no one before morning."

At the sound of a distant bell, Gage pulled out a golden pocket watch. "Just ten o'clock." He smiled across the table at his wife. "The troops are all at the bottom of the Common. They'll be stepping into the boats at any moment now, and the march will begin."

Still smiling, he unfolded the map which only Mrs. Gage and Lord Percy had been allowed to see. For the tenth time, his finger followed the line of march. The boats were to land at Lechmere Point, in Cambridge.

Staring at the spot on the map, Gage remembered what he'd told Colonel Smith.

"By ten, your men will all be at the bottom of the Common, ready to move. The boats will be drawn up. If any loiterers are nearby, send them packing. If they become difficult, arrest as many as you have to. No softness this time. On the stroke of ten, you are to begin ferrying the troops across. The operation must be carried out in complete silence.

"At Cambridge I will send you further marching orders. Until then, you will have one task, and one task only: to keep the men quiet, alert, and in place. There are few houses nearby, and the road is seldom traveled, but you must take no chances of being discovered."

Smith had been curious but had asked no questions. A fool, but a good soldier.

Gage's finger went back to the map. At an hour past midnight, the men would start moving by an unused path across the marshes, till they'd come to the old road, leading from Charlestown to the village of Menotomy. At Menotomy, a few rebel leaders would be captured while asleep. No disturbance.

The troops should reach Lexington about four —in the deep of night. Adams and Hancock would be taken without trouble. Officers had been sent in advance to make sure of that.

From Lexington a quick, six-mile march would take the troops into Concord. No drums, no fifes. That would come later. By the time the villagers opened their shutters to the morning sun, both bridges across the Concord River would be secured—to cut off the village from the north. The munitions would be quietly seized.

By eight in the morning, a messenger would be on his way with the news that the troops were parading back down the high road toward Boston. Fifing and drumming and singing the countryside to its knees!

"It's good to see you smile again," Mrs. Gage said. "But shouldn't you be getting some sleep? You can't keep up this pace."

"I *am* tired." He yawned, folded the map, and rose from the table. "But this is too great a night for sleeping."

"You've done everything one man could do.

Staying awake, now, won't help. The plan is so simple, how could it possibly miss?"

"Somehow I can't help feeling that this is the biggest hour of my life," the governor said. "All the mistakes and disappointments will be wiped away, and we'll soon have more honors than we ever dreamed of."

Hand in hand they walked to the window and looked out. "The King has sent cruel words to you," Mrs. Gage murmured. "There'll be other words now."

"The King was right. I *did* make mistakes. Not being careful enough was the worst mistake of all. You, better than anyone else, know what a year of disappointment and failure this has been. It seems every scheme I launched was turned against me.

"Adams and his Sons of Liberty have ears and eyes everywhere. Somehow they got to Portsmouth ahead of us and made me the laughing stock of the world. I gave orders to seize the munitions at Salem. Somehow the rebels reached the bridge at Salem ahead of us. The women jeered my name out of town.

"But not this time," he said. "This time it will be very different."

Mrs. Gage always became sleepy when her husband made a speech. She kissed him good night, and went to bed.

Smiling out at the city that had hurt him so, the city he would finally master, Gage recalled how Percy'd responded to the plan.

"Excellent!" the young lord had exclaimed. "You've worked out everything to perfection. I'm sure the troops will perform well."

Gage frowned, remembering Lord Percy's next words: "The news will become known after daybreak. What if some of the farmers are stupid enough to come running with their rusty rifles, while our troops march back to Boston?"

But he'd had a ready answer for Percy's doubts. "Smith has his orders: not to fire unless the rebels fire first. And I'll wager this gold watch there'll not be a shot fired. They've made plenty of fine battle speeches, but that's all the battling they'll do. They may shout insults—but our fifes and drums will be louder. We'll give them a show—real uniforms, real guns, real soldiers—a show they'll never forget."

Still, Percy hadn't been quite satisfied. The plan, he admitted, was perfect—on paper. "If nothing unexpected develops," he had said, "it will be a triumph for you, and will set back the Liberty crowd ten years. If . . ."

Then he had come out with a new objection. "Suppose Adams and Hancock are warned in time? Suppose they've got their militia, twice your number, waiting for Smith right now? Suppose they do open fire?"

Gage had smiled tolerantly. He smiled again now, remembering how he'd handled this question. "Impossible. Not *this* time. Boston's locked up tight as a drum. No rebel spy can get out of this town. If, by some miracle, messengers did manage to get through, our traps would gather them in, no matter what road they'd try to take. But who could know enough to warn them anyhow? Even Smith himself doesn't know. You and my wife are the only two people . . ."

Plainly, Percy had not been satisfied with the answer. "Still, Governor, we must cover every possibility. This is something like war. No trifling expedition. We must be ready to face any mishap."

"Exactly. And that's the reason I sent for you. If Smith runs into any trouble, I've promised that your men will reinforce him."

Gage pulled out his watch. Less than an hour had passed since he'd spoken to Percy. He looked out at the street and suddenly, he caught sight of a tall figure half-running toward Province House. The man took the steps two at a time, and knocked loudly.

A servant opened the door and the visitor flew upstairs without waiting to be announced.

Gage met him at the top of the stairs. "Percy! What's wrong?"

All the blood seemed to have left Lord Percy's face. He fell into a chair without bothering to remove hat or cloak. "'Impossible . . . you said . . . Even Smith doesn't know . . .'"

The governor sat down limply.

"Well, Governor, you don't have to worry about *me* giving your plan away. The whole city knows what you're up to."

In a voice that had sunk almost to a whisper, Percy told what had happened after he'd left Province House. He'd gone to watch the troops prepare to embark. It was dark as he crossed the Common. He was not recognized. "The British troops have marched, but will miss their aim," someone said, from the shadows. "What aim?" Percy had asked. The loiterers seemed surprised at his not knowing. "Why, the munitions at Concord!"

Gage leaped from the chair and paced from one end of the room to the other. "But how? How? How could anyone possibly know? In the whole world, only you and my wife saw that map! Can they pluck the thoughts out of a man's skull?"

Percy shrugged his shoulders. ". . . If I were you, Governor, I wouldn't waste a moment on *how* the plan became known. The important thing is what to do about it now. And," looking Gage straight in the eye, he went on, "if you'll forgive my frankness, you'd better not ask *how* tomorrow."

"What are you driving at?"

"Our men have been hearing rumors about your wife: being American-born, and all that . . . It would be too bad if they knew what happened to your secret."

Gage covered his face with his hands, fighting against the ugly thought. When he looked up again, he had the eyes and voice of a wounded man. "You don't believe such a thing, Percy?"

The young soldier shrugged once more. "As I said, you're wasting time with questions that may never be answered."

Gage drew himself up as though for battle, stalked to the window, and frowned out at Boston: "Not a man, woman, or child must be allowed to leave Boston tonight. The guard at the town gate must be doubled again. Every yard of shoreline must be patrolled. Anyone on the streets, not in uniform, must be stopped and searched."

He went over to Percy, and put a hand on his shoulder. "I leave this to you."

## DAY OF GLORY: *Eleven P.M.*

*W*hen the door of Warren's house closed behind him, a thought shot through Paul Revere's head: so much is planned for this night, both by our enemies and us. So much else may happen that nobody planned on; I wonder, Joseph, how things will be with us when we meet again—*if* we meet again.

But he let the thought go. He could not afford to take his mind off the work at hand, not even for a moment.

First, there was a certain street corner near Christ Church, where Robert Newman was waiting to be told that the British were moving and by water. That meant two lanterns must be hung from the steeple.

Across the river, in Charlestown, eyes would be fixed on Christ Church—watching for the signal. As soon as the lights went on, horses would be saddled. If Revere himself could not manage to get across, other messengers would be rushed off to tell Adams and Hancock that the troops had embarked.

When he'd finished with Newman, Revere had to get past the swarms of redcoats in North Square, put on his riding clothes, and say goodby to his wife. This part of the night's work would be the most difficult.

Not that Rachel wasn't used to it. Two years before, after the Boston Tea Party, there was a good-by they'd always remember. Paul had been chosen to bring the news to New York. Last year, in May, the news he had to carry was different: the port of Boston was being closed in revenge for the dumping of the tea. He had been sent all the way to Philadelphia, scattering printed copies of the hated Port Act wherever he went.

In September it had been Philadelphia again, bringing Dr. Warren's brave *Suffolk Resolves* to the Continental Congress. He'd carried home a promise from all America "that if the British troops in Boston should take the offensive, the other colonies would go to her help with armed force."

It was the parting last December that had been hardest for Paul and his wife to endure. Their son was only five days old. The Sons of Liberty discovered that Gage was sending a boatload of soldiers to Fort William and Mary in New Hampshire, to seize supplies and hold that fort. The patriots of New Hampshire had to be warned, and who but Revere could be depended on to travel sixty miles across snow and ice in less than a day?

A few days later he had returned to Boston with the news that the Americans—warned in time—had captured the fort, with 97 kegs of powder and 100 small arms! King George's rage had resulted in the order to capture all American supplies. Now, four months later, that command was being carried out.

There was no ice or snow on the roads now— it was fine traveling weather. This would be a short trip compared to the others. Yet, Revere and his wife knew this good-by was like none that had gone before.

"Wherever you're going, Paul, I'm sure it's right; and I won't try to stop you. But one thing —promise me—you'll be more careful!"

"You're not really afraid, Rachel?"

"It would be a lie to say I'm not afraid. This time, the British will shoot to kill. I can see it in their eyes. They'll be watching everywhere for you; they know who you are. You've got to watch for them, too. Remember, I want you home in one piece."

With the dog at his side, he left the house. He chose the darkest streets, so that no one would notice him in his short coat and heavy riding boots. Two Sons of Liberty, Joshua Bentley and Tom Richardson, were waiting to row him across the river. He found his friends in a dark hallway, just as they'd arranged. With the dog still tagging along, they hurried toward the spot where Revere kept his rowboat hidden.

Suddenly, he stopped in his tracks. "Devil take it! What's happening to my brain? I forgot the muffles for the oars."

"It's too late to turn back now," Bentley said. "We'll just have to take our chances."

Richardson scratched his head, then grinned. "I'll get the oars muffled—don't worry. Follow me!"

He led them to a house on the next street, and gave a funny, little whistle outside a certain window. The shutters flew open, and a young woman stuck her head out into the night. "That you, Tom?"

"Yes, don't *yell* so. Throw down a piece of cloth, anything, and don't ask why."

The head disappeared. A moment later a hand appeared, and a flannel petticoat was tossed down. Chuckling, they hurried on. But once again Revere stopped, and smashed his forehead with his hand.

"What else did you forget, Paul?"

"It's my wife's fault. I should never kiss her good-by." They laughed. "My spurs—believe it or not—I forgot my spurs!"

How could he get them? It would be madness to risk going back through the guarded streets. The dog looked at him, and he looked at the dog. Swiftly he scribbled a note to Rachel, and tied it to the animal's collar. Luckily, the British were not yet searching and questioning dogs. In a few minutes, Rover was back with the spurs.

Now they must really hurry. Without a sound, they got into the boat and pulled away from shore. If anything else had been forgotten, it would be just too bad. If anything should be said, it would just have to wait.

How impossibly distant the lights of Charlestown seemed! There, beside them, blocking the mouth of the river, sat the British man-of-war, the *Somerset*. In the moonlight the ship glittered like an armored ghost. How many eyes sought them from that silent monster?

One thing the men knew for certain, as they rowed noiselessly farther and farther from shore: the great ship was there only to block them, discover them, and destroy them.

They tried to keep out of the range of the moon. The slightest splash of an oar, a whisper, would be enough to do them in. Each moment they expected lanterns to flash on their faces, a whistle to rip through the night, a reception committee of pistols.

Bentley and Richardson saw nothing but the shore they'd left, perhaps for the last time. Revere saw nothing but the shore they wanted to, had to, reach—and perhaps never would.

At last one of them dared to look over his shoulder. The *Somerset* was far behind, a little toy in the moonlight! Somehow they'd managed to slip by, and Charlestown loomed near. In a moment the boat struck sand.

From the windows of Colonel Conant's house, Boston, and the high steeple of Christ Church could be seen clearly. Neither the sixty-four cannon of the *Somerset,* nor the doubled guard at the town gate, would be able to hold back the signaled news: which way the British were coming, and when.

The door opened. Inside, a group of patriots talked nervously. At the sight of Paul on the threshold, the air became electric. "Revere! How'd you make it, you rascal?"

"I knew he'd get across! Didn't I offer to wager on it?"

One of them dragged him to a chair. "Here! Let the man catch his breath!"

Another brought a cup of water, which Paul gulped down gratefully. "Did you see the lanterns?"

"We certainly did—clearer than stars!"

He jumped up. "The troops must all be over by now. I'd better get saddled and go."

The smile disappeared from Conant's face. "The horse is ready. Will you watch yourself every step of the way this time, Paul? The roads are full of patrols."

They turned to Revere—Revere of the dark face and eyes, Revere of the hair, unpowdered and unwigged. They'd all known him for years as master goldsmith, silversmith, coppersmith, engraver: as express messenger. "Bold Revere," ready to answer back any royal governor, "Cool Revere," ready to do simply, quietly, whatever had to be done. It was his turn to speak.

The voice was full and firm. "With a good horse and a bit of luck I'll get through."

## DAY OF GLORY: *Midnight*

*J*ohn Larkin, one of the wealthiest men in Charlestown, had offered the finest horse in his stable: a graceful, sure-footed mount, that stamped its small hoofs impatiently. As soon as he was sure of the bit and stirrups, Paul mounted and galloped away. He looked back only once at the lighted doorway from which his friends were waving.

He passed through Charlestown Neck and was now in a deserted section of open fields, marshes

and clay ponds. Of the two roads crossing this
gloomy region, Revere decided to take the one on
the left, which was little used but was the short-
est way to Lexington.

With so little time, he could hardly keep himself from riding at full speed. But he remembered
that the road would be alive with British officers.
He held the horse in check, so it would have
enough wind left to fly forward or wheel back in
case of trouble.

Suddenly, just ahead, in a narrow part of the
winding road, he noticed two figures on horseback, under a tree. The moon gave them away.
They were British officers—he could make out the
cockades on their hats.

At the same instant, they'd seen him, too. One
of them started his horse toward Revere, and the
other galloped up the road to cut off the American if he should get past the first.

But Revere swiftly turned his horse and flew
at full gallop through the marshes, with one of
the officers close behind.

Now, for the first time, the slender animal
could prove how good it really was. Not a shot
was fired, not a word spoken—the one rider could
think only of escaping, the other of overtaking.
Out of the corner of his eye Revere saw that the
heavy British steed was beginning to lose ground.

For three hundred yards the savage race went

on. Then, all at once, there was a loud thud, and a muttered oath. Without slowing, Revere raised himself in his stirrups and looked back. His pursuer had got himself stuck in the very clay pond Revere had been so careful to bypass! He galloped on through the marshlands till he reached the main road.

While Revere sped forward in the moonlight—warning every household that the British were coming—the same moon, on another road, was playing another kind of trick.

Very slowly, very quietly, the nine officers Solomon Brown had met at sunset went jogging along the roads farther and farther away from Boston, deeper into the night.

So far, Major Mitchell felt, the operation was going well. Now it was drawing close to midnight, and the officers were becoming impatient. The pleasantness of the early evening had given way to a frightening gloom.

It had been easy enough for the governor to say: "Avoid the settlements—keep in the shadows of the pasturelands."

"But," they mumbled to one another, "would Gage himself be more comfortable than we are in this dark and silent place?"

They *must* find the Clark house, and soon. It was the task of these carefully picked men to

search out the Clark house for Smith's army, or—
if they could manage it alone—take prisoner the
Massachusetts delegates to Philadelphia: Sam
Adams and John Hancock.

When they finally entered Lexington, they
were startled to see so many lanterns burning,
and the tavern still crowded. Mitchell decided
that it would be suicide to ask about the Clark
house, or even to loiter long in Lexington. Glad to
have passed through without being noticed, they
rode beyond the village along the Concord road.

A mile or so out of Lexington, seeing that the
country was deserted, Major Mitchell drew rein.
"We'll wait here," he whispered. "It's dark
enough. In an hour, we'll go back. By then, everyone will be in bed."

The officer who'd been riding in the rear
thought this would be a good time to tell them
what had been bothering him for three or four
miles. "A few times I thought I heard horses close
behind me."

"Nonsense!" one of the others responded.
"You've been hearing our horses for so many
hours, it's gone to your head."

But Mitchell wasn't taking any chances. Gage
had told him yesterday, "Be *careful*, every inch
of the way!"

"If you think we're being followed," he said,
"here's what we'll do. We'll set out again toward

Concord. As soon as we come to an especially dark spot, the four front riders will turn off the road and wait behind the trees. That way we'll find out if we're being followed."

They pushed slowly forward. Just ahead, the road was lined on both sides by elms, stretching their huge arms toward one another until they met and intertwined so that scarcely a beam of moonlight could push through.

Shielded by darkness and by the officers behind them, Mitchell and his three foremost riders turned off the road and vanished behind the elms. The others continued straight ahead as though nothing had happened.

They did not have long to wait in ambush. A sound of hoofs was soon heard, growing steadily louder. In a few moments, three horsemen came into view. By the way all three craned their necks forward and kept exactly the same pace as those ahead, it was clear that their object was to follow the British.

Mitchell waited until they'd passed; then he led his men back onto the road so that they blocked it from end to end. He pointed his pistol to the sky and fired once.

At this signal, the officers ahead wheeled sharply and tore down on the horsemen. Not knowing they'd been trapped, the Americans turned and started back toward Lexington. They found themselves face to face with a line of pistols.

"Stop or we'll blow you to bits! Following us, were you? We'll teach you to keep your bedtime hours! What were you up to, ha? Who sent you?" At each question, a slap across the face.

"None of that, men!" the major barked. "You'll never get an answer out of them that way. Let's take them off the road into this pasture. It's much brighter there. I want to look them over."

They were mere boys. They'd plainly been surprised. But was it fright or stubbornness that tied their tongues?

"Now, lads," Mitchell began softly, "you needn't act as if you expected to be eaten alive. We're officers of the King, and mean you no harm. Understand? First of all, what are your names?"

"Elijah Sanderson." "Jonathan Loring." "Solomon Brown."

"You can speak. Fine. Now—where are you from?"

"Lexington."

"Lexington . . . you've had big men there these past days."

Solomon appeared puzzled. "Big men?"

"Don't tell me you haven't heard—" he searched their faces, clear in the moonlight, "about Adams and Hancock being at Clark's?"

Their faces told him nothing.

"It really would be worth your while to tell me how I can find them. The governor needs their help right away, and has an important message for them."

The Yankees sat still and looked stupid.

"We'll be heading back for Lexington very soon," Mitchell continued, beginning to lose patience, "and you'll show us where the Clark house is. Then you can go home."

"I was at the Clark house this evening, sir," Solomon answered. "Nobody was there but the parson and his family. Those men you want must be somewhere else. Have you tried Burlington . . . ?"

The major frowned. "What were you doing on the road?" Silence. "*Well—what were you doing?*" His voice became harder. "Who told you to follow us? You might as well tell, because I know."

At a nod from Mitchell, three officers closed in on the boys and grabbed them each by the collar.

"They may change their minds after a while, and decide to be more helpful. Remember," Mitchell whispered, "no blood! Threaten, but *no blood!*"

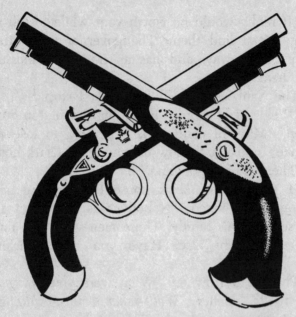

## DAY OF GLORY: *One A.M.*

*T*wo hours before, the last of his men had been sent off, and Warren had said good night to his servant, Boston John. Now, tossing from side to side, he tried to sleep. Here it was—already one o'clock.

A few times he'd dozed off—only to wake more exhausted than ever. First in a half dream—he'd imagined that the messenger, William Dawes, was stopped at the town gate, and dragged away to Province House for questioning. Then he dreamed that his other rider, Revere, was caught by a *Somerset* patrol while crossing the river.

The last dream was the longest, and the most terrifying. Sam Adams was asleep in the Clark house. Neither messenger had gotten through to warn him. Slowly, up the road toward Lexington, a great army of redcoats moved. Every household along the way slept.

Now they were entering the village, pushing toward the Clark house, surrounding it with a thousand pistols. Now they were at the door of Adams' room. The moon touched his face—that pale, thin face on which all of Boston's suffering and splendor were recorded. The door was flung open—redcoats burst in.

Warren tore himself loose from the nightmare, and jumped out of bed. Back and forth he paced, mumbling to himself: "And if Dawes, if Revere, did get through, if they did reach Lexington in time—would it be worth the trouble? Would Adams listen to the plea that he and Hancock hide somewhere as far from Lexington as possible?

"Or would he still be at the Clark house, joining Revere in a cup of tea, scolding me for having risked the capture of two messengers just to save one old man? Would he politely excuse himself and go back to sleep?

"Sam . . . Sam . . . what's to become of our cause without you? And I—what will I be without you, father and friend? If only I'd gone myself! You might've listened to me, and let me drag you away to a safe place before it would be too late . . . Too late! One o'clock . . . it's too late now for me to do anything but sleep. In an hour or two the whole affair will be settled. . . ."

Ashamed of himself for being safe at home, the doctor once more went to bed. He didn't know that downstairs Boston John sat beside the door —with a loaded musket in his lap.

Warren was not the only one in Boston who dreamed about Samuel Adams that night. Half a mile or so away, in Province House, Governor Gage had gone to bed full of doubts after Percy's second visit. Over and over he'd asked his wife to try to remember—perhaps, accidentally, she'd let the secret slip out.

Over and over the answer had come: "No . . . of course not! You told me not to, so I didn't. Those people on the Common were only guessing. After all, they could see the troops and the boats, so they guessed Concord. Get to sleep now."

The comforting voice had helped. In no time at all he was asleep, and dreaming.

In his dream Gage found himself in a huge courtroom in London. A trial was almost ready to begin. Neither judge nor prisoner could be seen, but already every public seat was taken.

A great murmur arose as two of the other witnesses filed in. One was Bernard, the other Hutchinson. Both had been governors of Massachusetts —two splendid men, driven like dogs from the streets of Boston!

They gripped his hand. "Excellent work, Governor! You certainly turned the trick!" Hutchinson beamed. "Britain will be grateful to your forever, and the colonies, too."

All at once the courtroom became hushed. Flanked by two powerful guards, Samuel Adams was brought in. How puny he showed himself to be—not at all the giant he'd seemed in Boston! The guards shoved him so that he half fell onto the prisoner's bench.

Now the judge, in wig and long black robe, stalked in and took his place at the center of the stage. He began unrolling an endless scroll, and shook his head hopelessly.

"Samuel Adams, you are charged with so many monstrous acts against the Crown, that it would take a day and night to read through the list. I shall therefore read the last passage only, to which you can plead guilty or not guilty:

" 'In view of the above rebellious acts which are common knowledge, the prosecutor must charge Samuel Adams of Massachusetts with high treason against the King. His aim has been to so inflame the King's subjects in the colonies, that

the lawful government would be overthrown!
Samuel Adams, you've heard the charges—how
do you plead?"

From every part of the courtroom cries could
be heard: "Guilty! Hang the traitor!"

Gage stirred in his sleep. The man who rose to
speak had a green face, like Satan. The voice was
harsh and grating—Adams' own voice. "How can
I plead, without first hearing what acts I'm accused of? Would your Lordship let me hear the
list?"

"He's playing for time!" someone roared. "We
know him! We know the list! To the gallows!"

But the Court had to show it was just. In all
his dignity the judge spoke: "The prisoner's re-
quest is granted. Read the list."

The prosecutor stepped forward, took the scroll,
and read: "Of the years before 1765, much can
be told—but it was in that year truly that the
treason of Samuel Adams ripened for all to see.
In that year, he was responsible for the hanging
of an effigy of His Majesty's collector of the Stamp
Tax, Andrew Oliver, from a branch of the so-called
Liberty Tree. He forced Mr. Oliver to appear
before two thousand Sons of Liberty and take an
oath never to sell a stamp.

"During the next two years, the accused was
content to write articles against the Crown. These

evil seeds took root, and bloomed: more burnings, more hangings in effigy.

"It was in 1769 he sent forth a lying report against the conduct of the King's troops in Boston. A year later, Samuel Adams organized that entire unfortunate incident which is now known as the Boston Massacre. He used the shooting down of a few troublemakers to further his plan of separating the colonies from the Mother Country. By forcing two regiments to quit Boston, he left the town at the mercy of his mobs.

"In 1772 he formed a monstrous plan of letter-writing, called the Committee of Correspondence, by which the troublemakers of one province could disclose to rebels in other provinces what new plots were under way. The following year he personally plotted and organized the Boston Tea Party. He led the town of Boston in its stubborn refusal to pay for the tea that was destroyed.

"It was in 1773, as well, that he called for a congress of all the colonies, where he could sow his seeds of treason throughout America.

"He made the closing of the port an excuse to arouse the whole continent to make the cause of Boston its own. He got himself elected as one of the Massachusetts delegates, to an unlawful congress in Philadelphia. Last year, too, the prisoner set forth his plan of arming the rebels in every town and village, forming them into military companies. . . ."

Before the prosecutor could begin listing the traitorous acts of Sam Adams in 1775, Gage woke from the dream, shaking with excitement. These last events the governor knew too well. How many sleepless nights they had caused him!

Even after he realized that it had been only a dream, that this was not London, that the great trick had not yet been pulled off, Gage enjoyed the memory of Adams in chains.

And perhaps Adams had already been made prisoner! What time was it, anyway? He lit a candle and fumbled for his watch. "One o'clock! The men should be lined up in ranks, ready for the signal to march. Smith is galloping from one end of the line to the other, making sure that everything's in order. Now, he's taking his place at the head of the troops. Now, the signal . . ."

Gage slipped his watch back into its pocket and blew out the light.

## DAY OF GLORY: *Two A.M.*

At midnight, the men on guard at the Clark house had been startled by a loud galloping. They were sure it was Solomon Brown or one of the others, bringing important news. The horseman came straight to the door, and dismounted. It was a man none of them knew. They covered him with their muskets, and Sergeant Munroe blocked the door.

"Let me pass!" roared the stranger. "I've no time for games!"

Monroe noticed the windblown hair, the sweating forehead. "Please, sir, whoever you are—try to control your voice. The ladies and gentlemen have all gone to bed. It's been a tiring day, and they've requested not to be disturbed by any noise."

"Noise!" the stranger shouted. "You'll have noise enough before long. The Regulars are out."

At these words, the musket almost dropped out of Munroe's hand. A window opened, and Reverend Clark called, "What is it, lads?"

"I must speak with John Hancock."

From the window it was impossible to make out the stranger's face. "I'm sorry sir. I can't be opening the door at this time of night."

Hancock had gone to bed, but was not yet asleep. He recognized the voice booming through the quiet night and hurried down to open the door. "Come in, Revere!"

Immediately the household was in an uproar. Everyone raced downstairs.

"I saw the British at ten, ferrying across the Charles," Revere said. "Maybe a thousand. They might be here at any moment. Dr. Warren thinks their aim is to pick up you two and send you back to Gage in chains—then move on to Concord for our guns and powder. Will Dawes should've been here ahead of me—Warren sent him by land an hour earlier . . . I hope he wasn't caught."

They made Revere sit down and take some food and drink. While he ate, Revere followed the argument that was going on between Hancock and Adams.

"Bring me my sword and gun!" Hancock kept shouting, as he paraded back and forth in his fine silk gown and slippers. "I'm of this village as much as anyone else. If the Minute Men of Lexington are going out to meet the redcoats face to face, how can I not be among them?"

Adams quietly answered, "What sense would there be in that, John? We all know you're a brave fellow, ready to risk your life for liberty. But isn't that just what Gage would like most?"

"No—don't try to argue—" Hancock shook his head firmly. "You must leave without me, Sam. I'm a colonel—my work is here. You're too old for guns; nobody expects you to be a soldier. Besides, they'll need you in Philadelphia, much more than they need me. No—I'll stay right here with my boys, and beat the troops back to Boston."

This was becoming serious. Adams stopped smiling. "Listen to me, John Hancock! When the time comes for shooting, I'll manage to keep up with you. But you and I have other things to worry about, tonight. The citizens of Massachusetts chose us to speak for them in Philadelphia. Where are we to be next month, you and I? Chained, in London, as Gage hopes, or battling for liberty in Philadelphia? To stay here is to be caught."

Half an hour had passed. Then a sound of hoofs, and Dawes was outside, knocking. What a relief to see the Boston cordwainer safe and sound! He had come by back roads and had aroused every household on the way. Minute Men, near and far, were by now wide awake, polishing their guns.

The two riders decided to go on, as quickly as possible, and alarm the people of Concord. It would be bad if the redcoats fell upon the town without warning. In a savage mood, there was no telling what these troops might do.

It was after one o'clock when Revere and Dawes reached the main road and headed for Concord. Suddenly, a galloping was heard behind them; and a lively voice called out. "Hello, there —wait for me!"

They let the rider overtake them. He turned out to be a young Concord doctor, Samuel Prescott. He had somehow missed the general alarm and when they told him who they were, and what they were up to, he was greatly excited.

"Most of the supplies which Gage expected to find are hidden," Prescott said, "but some cannon and other heavy equipment has been left in the village. Could you stand my company from here to Concord?"

They were happy to have him. Revere explained that they meant to alarm every house on the way—but quietly, keeping on the lookout for British patrols.

"Excellent," the doctor agreed. "And since everyone between here and Concord knows me, there'll be no trouble getting them to open their shutters and believe the news."

The work went well. Before long, the three had reached the halfway point between Lexington and Concord. While Prescott and Dawes stopped at a certain house, Revere went on, peering through the darkness to see if the road was safe.

He'd gone about two hundred yards, when he noticed two British officers on horseback—huddled in the shadow of a tree. It was very much like the scene on the Charlestown road, three hours earlier. This time, though, Paul Revere was more amused than frightened.

"Come up, men!" he yelled back. "Here's two of them!" Instantly, he realized that he'd committed a real blunder. There were four of the enemy, not two! Before he could try to turn his horse, they had him surrounded and were pointing their pistols at his head.

"Devil take you! If you go an inch further," said a low voice, "you are a dead man."

Before Revere could cry out a warning, Prescott and Dawes galloped up. Prescott, being in front, was at once covered by the British guns. As soon as Dawes understood what was going on, he turned his horse and raced away. Two of the officers chased after him. Leaving the road, he headed cross-country straight for a deserted farmhouse, the officers close behind him.

When he reached the empty house, he yelled as loud as he could. "Halloo, my boys! I've got two of 'em!"

Not knowing that Billy Dawes was a born actor, the officers really believed he'd led them into ambush. They wheeled around and fled.

It was lucky for their fellow officers that they returned so soon. The two remaining prisoners were making a lot of mischief. It took the four, with pistols and swords, to keep Revere and Prescott from getting away.

There was an opening on one side of the road, leading into a pasture. The bars had been taken down, and now the officers drove their prisoners into the pasture like cattle.

No sooner were they inside, with the bars back in place, than Prescott cried, "Put on!" and swerved to the left. Before anyone could stop him, he crossed the pasture, jumped his horse over a low stone wall, and vanished.

While dazed eyes followed the young doctor, Revere broke away and raced toward a wood at the bottom of the pasture. His plan was to dismount and escape on foot through the woods. However, just as he reached the trees, five other Britishers seized his bridle, put their pistols to his breast, and ordered him to dismount.

One of them, who seemed to be in charge, behaved more civilly than the others. "Where are you from?" he asked.

"Boston."

"What time did you leave it?"

"About eleven."

At this, the officer turned with a look of surprise, to his men. Then, showing new interest, he studied the prisoner's face. "Sir, may I ask your name?"

"My name is Revere."

Once more the officers gave each other a meaningful look. "What!" the questioner exclaimed, "*Paul* Revere?"

"Yes."

One of the officers rushed forward. "Let me at him!"

"So that's what the rascal looks like!" another jeered, pushing his nose into Revere's face. "Not much; a Yankee bumpkin like all the rest."

"Don't be afraid, Revere," their leader said.

With a smile that kept growing broader, Revere looked the man straight in the eye. "*I* afraid? There's nothing for me to be afraid of, sir. It's you who'd better watch out."

One of the British was about to answer with the butt of his pistol. The leader held him back. "What did you mean by that?"

"I mean, sir, that you're going to miss your aim."

"What aim? It happens that we're to catch some deserters down this road."

Revere laughed in his face. "Deserters? Is that what you've been telling people? Well, don't bother telling me your fairy tales. I know what you're after." Realizing that his only chance of escape would be by putting a scare into them, he went on: "Your boats are catch'd aground; and we'll have five hundred men in Lexington before the next hour strikes."

They whispered together. Revere heard the leader mumble: "It *could* be the truth. You'd better bring Mitchell here at once!"

## DAY OF GLORY: *Three A.M.*

*M*ajor! Major!" even before he'd reached the
road, the officer called out: "Major Mitchell!
Quickly!"

"Yes! What is it now?" Mitchell answered in a
biting voice. For the past hour the major had been
getting more and more impatient, snapping at
anyone who tried to speak. The night was rushing past, yet here he was—guarding three useless
boys from Lexington who said nothing half the
time, and told lies the other half. He knew as lit-

tle of Hancock's and Adams' whereabouts as before.

For a moment, when the dark Boston man had
fallen into the trap and had led his friends in after
him, Mitchell felt the night's work was not altogether wasted. At least he'd kept them from
reaching Concord. But when one, then another,
escaped, there was no limit to his rage.

His anger had not yet spent itself, when he
heard his name called from the pasture. "What is
it? What is it?"

Breathlessly, the officer told him who it was
they'd captured, and repeated Revere's terrifying
words.

"The fellow's lying," Mitchell broke in. "Can't
you see he's trying to save his skin?" All the same,
the news rocked him. He galloped toward the
wood where the prisoners were being held: Revere, grinning at his captors; and the lads of Lexington watching from the bushes.

The major went straight toward Revere and
clapped his pistol to the Boston man's head. "I'm
going to ask you some questions, Revere. If you
don't tell the truth I'll put a bullet through your
skull."

Revere nodded with mock politeness. "I am a
man of truth, sir. You stopped me on the public
highway, and made me a prisoner, I know not by

what right. You'll get the truth from me—I'm not afraid."

The major fired questions at him and Revere gave the same answers as before. Although the pistol was pointed at the American's head, it was the Britisher who mopped the sweat off his brow and stammered so that he swallowed a question without asking it.

"Mount your horse!" he finally ordered, after searching the prisoner for weapons. When Revere had mounted, the major tore the reins out of his hand. "You are not to ride with reins!"

"I won't run from you."

"Indeed, you won't," answered Mitchell, giving the reins over to one of the lieutenants. Then he remembered Solomon Brown and the others. "All right, you three! Get out of the bushes, and mount your horses!" Turning to Revere, he warned: "We're returning to Lexington and if you try to run, or insult us, I swear we'll blow your brains out."

At the road, the officers formed a circle, with the prisoners in the center, and Revere in front. Neither his own men, nor the prisoners, could see the frown of worry on Major Mitchell's face in the darkness. Too much of what Revere told him sounded true. He should have realized as much, when they passed the Lexington tavern close to midnight and saw that it was crowded. When he discovered the young rebels following him . . .

Adams and Hancock had no doubt been warned, and were probably far away by now. There was only one task left: to join Smith before the country was roused and they, themselves, were cut off. If his mission had been a failure so far, at least he could warn Smith that the Yankees were neither asleep nor afraid. Gage had been wrong to say the rebels would not fight. It was possible, now, that more than one shot might have to be fired before the night's work was done.

They rode swiftly, but not so swiftly that they neglected to threaten Revere all the way. "You know," said the officer who guarded him, "you're in a pretty serious position."

"I'm sensible of it," the prisoner replied.

It was now close to three o'clock. Hardly a sound could be heard, except for the hoofs of their horses. An officer still held the reins of Revere's horse. He had orders to shoot if Revere made a break for freedom. Suddenly, when they were only about half a mile from the village, a shot rang out and echoed across the countryside. Mitchell dashed forward.

"What was that?" he barked to Revere.

"That? Just a signal to alarm the country."

At these words the major wheeled around and ordered a halt. "Get off your horses," he said to the Lexington boys. He cut the bridles and saddles, and drove the animals away. Then he muttered, "You three go about your business."

"Can I go, too?" Revere quickly asked.

"Oh no, not you, Revere. I'll take you with me to Boston, no matter what." Once more he gave the order to ride on.

They were now so close to Lexington, they could see the Meeting House silhouetted against the moon. A volley of guns sounded. The horses drew back in alarm.

Again, the major ordered a halt. His voice had suddenly lost all of its bullying power. "How far is it to Cambridge?"

"Maybe ten miles."

"Is there any other road?"

"None that I know of," Revere lied.

The major consulted in a whisper with some of his men. Then he rode up to the man who was guarding Revere. "Is your horse tired?"

"Yes, it is."

"Then take Revere's. Cut your bridle and saddle, let your nag go."

They galloped away without once looking back, leaving Revere by the side of the road.

A half-hour later, riding toward Lexington at the head of his army, Colonel Smith gave a muffled oath. Something had clearly gone wrong. According to Gage's plan, Mitchell's men were

supposed to be at Lexington right now. Yet here
they were, headed for Boston, their wigs flapping
in a crazy lopsided dance—looking for all the
world as if they were pursued by ghosts.

Smith was impatient at this new delay. He was
already more than an hour behind schedule, and
still miles away from Lexington.

It had been easy for Gage to sketch arrows on
a piece of paper—but the governor himself had
never known what it was like to push across a
wilderness, or wade through the freezing water of
salt marshes.

"Mitchell! What are *you* doing here?" Smith
called out.

"The whole country's alarmed, Colonel! We galloped for our lives!" The officer told about the
prisoners he'd taken, and what Paul Revere had
said, and how the guns had been fired at Lexington. "Before we were out of that place, we could
hear the bells ringing, and the drums beating to
arms, and all the other villages answering. I
swear, sir, you'd better send for Percy! There's
five hundred waiting for you already, with more
rebels pouring in from the country every minute."

Now Smith understood what had happened a
few miles back. At Menotomy, following Gage's
instructions, he'd detached a squad to seize certain rebel leaders.

The house had been searched from top to bottom—but the Americans were nowhere to be found. Three beds were still warm—the covers had clearly been flung aside in haste; and clothing was found which the leaders had had no time to put on.

It seemed strange: the troops had moved quite noiselessly, and could not possibly be accused of waking the rebels. Then, too, there had been the sound of distant bells in the middle of the night —but he'd not paid much attention to them.

Now he knew who had given the warning. The rascal, Paul Revere, of course, passing by on his way to Lexington, must have made sure to stop and give the alarm. But how did Revere himself get through all the traps? Someone would have to answer that question.

Not now, though! Mitchell was right. A messenger must be sent to Gage at once. There might be bloody business. Who could say how many Americans were waiting to welcome them?

Smith hated to call for help; but his own skin was at stake. Glory would have to wait for another time.

By the time a messenger was dispatched with a note, Major Pitcairn had come up to find out what the trouble was. Pitcairn was an officer in the Marines. Bold and dashing, he had volunteered for this expedition.

"Major Pitcairn!" Smith exclaimed. "I want you to go ahead quickly with six light companies, and seize the two bridges at Concord. Mitchell, you go along. If you run into trouble, I'll be right behind you. I've just sent for reinforcements, so you can be sure we'll be well covered."

For a moment the major was too stunned to speak. His round, wide-eyed face suddenly seemed long and old. Was the colonel expecting him to march six light companies right through those five hundred at Lexington and go on to take the bridges at Concord? How would Smith like to do it himself?

"Any questions, Major?" Smith asked.

The major knew he had no one to blame but himself. He'd been mad to come on this adventure. "Fiery" and "gallant" everyone called him—and so he'd jumped at a chance to prove himself again. Swallowing his distrust of the drum-filled night, he murmured, "No, sir, no questions at all."

## DAY OF GLORY: *Four A.M.*

Solomon Brown stood in the moonlit road with his two friends. He could scarcely move. He listened, unbelieving, to the song of young crickets and the murmur of young leaves. The British, with their prisoner, Paul Revere, had vanished in the darkness. Their horses could no longer be heard.

No matter what else might happen to them, either this night or the rest of their lives, Solomon knew that neither he nor his companions would ever forget these past three hours. How close they'd come to death, with the icy stare of pistols! How close they'd stood to glory, with Revere's brave words and laughter echoing across the pasture! And their own silence, their own answers—how surprising! How suddenly they'd come into manhood!

"What are we standing here for?" Jonathan Loring whispered. "Let's get home!"

Solomon nodded. Then he said, with a new firmness, "Not by the road—next time we're taken, it mightn't end this easy."

They cut through the woods, leaping over brooks and briars, running, stumbling, out of breath, but never really stopping until they got to the Clark house.

Munroe and his guard were still on patrol. "Hallo, there!" he shouted.

At the door, the three lads caved in, unable to answer. Finally, after Dolly revived them with tea and biscuits, the story of their capture came out. Paul Revere, they said, hadn't been as lucky. As far as they knew he was still in British hands. But what a lesson in bravery Paul Revere had given the redcoats!

While they spoke, the express rider walked in. "*Revere!*" they cried out in relief. "How did you escape?"

He opened his mouth to answer, but when he saw that Adams and Hancock were still there, he

blurted out impatiently: *"What are you two doing
here?"* The room was electrified. Revere was only
an express rider. He'd never spoken to his chiefs
that way before.

"Warren stuck his neck out, and stayed in Boston, just so that he could find things out and
warn you in time. He sent Billy Dawes and me;
we stuck our necks out, too; he sent us just so
that we could warn you. These three lads, here,
went out on the road, got themselves trapped, just
so they could give you warning. Do you think it's
brave of you to be sitting here? Does it make
sense?"

Dolly clapped her hands together. "Bravo!
Bravo, Mr. Revere! I've been wanting to say exactly that for the past three hours. Whose fault do
you think it is? I give you one guess. Yes, it's
John Hancock, as usual. Don't think the parson
and Mr. Adams haven't tried to move him, but
he's more stubborn than a mule. He simply won't
budge. Look at him!"

Everyone turned to Hancock. There he was,
on the sofa, cleaning his gun and sword though
they needed no cleaning.

"The men of Lexington have decided what
they're going to do," he said. "They're going to
form their lines on the Green and face the Regulars. It's possible the soldiers will parade right by.
But what if they fire? Half our men never fought

before—oh yes, they're good at hunting deer or wild turkey. But these are the King's best troops they'll be facing. They need experienced men to stand beside them."

The room was silent. Hancock looked around, then went on. "How do you think I'll be able to live after this, if I turn my back on the British now? 'Here was the enemy'—people will say—'and here was the American colonel, right here where his father was born.' Shall they say I ran at the first sign of trouble; that John Hancock ran away from Lexington?"

"All these years," Revere answered, looking straight at Hancock, "we Sons of Liberty have played a trick that has sent more than one great governor packing. *Whatever they aimed for, we gave them just the opposite.* They sent troops to frighten Boston, so Boston frightened the troops out of their wits. They tried to dump their tea down our throats, so we dumped their tea in the ocean."

He walked over to the sofa and gently took the sword out of Hancock's hand. "Now they aim to snatch you, our leaders, before you can get to Philadelphia, to hang you in London as a lesson for the rest. Well, there's only one trick to answer that aim: we must send them back empty-handed! Let their night's work fail and another great governor will be on his way home to King George!"

Hancock stood up and sorrowfully laid aside his gun. The two leaders quickly packed and, with Paul Revere, set out for Woburn.

Before their carriage rolled away, the parson came out to give the patriot leaders his blessing. Dolly came out, too. She was still angry with Hancock for his stubborn delay—for what seemed a childish desire to prove his bravery. Yet—she came out in the night to stand beside the carriage.

"You'll join us later, and come to Philadelphia, my dear," John said.

"Shall I?" She looked up mischievously.

The horse started forward, and her voice followed him into the darkness that was just beginning to lift. "Remember, Mr. Hancock, I'm not under your control *yet*. I shall go to my father tomorrow." But when the carriage was almost out of sight, she waved good-by to it, and threw a kiss. Then she lifted her skirts daintily over the dewy grass, and hurried into the house.

When Solomon had galloped in from Boston with his news about the officers on the road, Captain Parker had immediately called out the Minute Men. Thirty Lexington farmers showed up. Since the evening was cold, they decided to wait around the fire at Buckman's Tavern.

At two o'clock, Parker had called the roll of his company, and ordered every man to load his gun.

For a while, they paraded around the Green, firing a few volleys. They sent a scout toward Boston. He came back with the report that he hadn't seen or heard any sign of a British Army. Nor had he seen the patrol. The boys were probably circling the fields or maybe they'd gone home to bed.

"There'll be no redcoats marching this far," Daniel Harrington said. "Gage is just trying to outfox us. He must have some other plan up his sleeve."

This made sense. Besides, the night was now really cold.

"The company's dismissed," Parker said, "but we'll keep sending scouts out and I want everyone to stay ready. Be prepared to assemble again at the beat of the drum!"

A few who lived very close to the Green had gone home, but most of the men had returned to Buckman's Tavern. They'd been sitting here for over an hour, when the door opened, and the missing patrol walked in.

"Hello! Look who's here! We gave you up for dead hours ago. What happened?"

From Solomon's report it was clear that the British were probably very close by now. It also seemed that the enemy expected to meet five hundred Minute Men in Lexington, and that the

American gunfire an hour before had thrown a scare into the officers.

A rider galloped up to the door. It was the scout, sent out twenty minutes before.

They crowded around him. "Did you see something?"

"*I* didn't at first—but the horse did. About a mile and a half down the road he suddenly stopped, and wouldn't go on. Then I saw two redcoats sitting very still, close to the fence. They didn't take any notice of me, so I tried to get the horse amoving. But neither whip nor spur could budge him.

"All of a sudden, what do I see? About twenty rods down the road, where it curves, along comes a whole army of redcoats. I turned right around, and this time it was no trouble getting the horse to move. He would've come right through the tavern if I hadn't reined him."

The time had come. Parker thought for a moment, then rose and quieted his company. "Men! Now we know it's true, and we know it's near. They expect guns to meet them on the Green of our village. Shall we run home while there's still time?"

"No!" The farmers roared with one voice.

"Shall we make a stand on our Green?"

"Yes! Why ask? We decided that before."

"But it was dark then, and the question began

with *If*. Now the night's lifting—whoever stands will be seen—and there's no *If* about the redcoats on the road."

"Let them see us!" the men shouted. "It was daylight in Salem when the people blocked the bridge. Are we less than the women of Salem?"

Sergeant Munroe and his seven men joined the group pouring out of the tavern. Now that Adams and Hancock were gone, there was no need to guard the Clark house. They were ready for new instructions.

"Sergeant Munore!" Parker ordered. "Form the company in two ranks, just north of the Meeting House. Now, man, fire the alarm guns! That's it. Again! Now, William," he smiled at the boy who hadn't left his side all night, "William Diamond, this is your time. Let's hear that drum of yours beat to arms! Louder! That's it. Louder! Let Gage hear it in Boston! Louder! Let the Ministers hear it in London!"

The men were by now formed in line. They marched solemnly behind the drummer, out onto the Green.

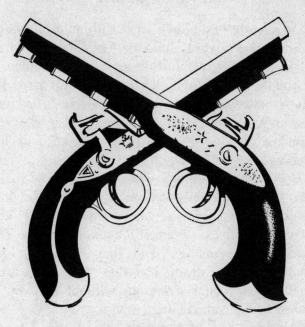

## DAY OF GLORY: *Five A.M.*

*A*ll at once, like a bird song in early morning, the shrill notes of a fife could be heard not far away. The men turned to see who it was. At least nine of them—Harrington's: brothers, cousins, sons —knew for certain who it was. They knew it was that other, that sixteen-year-old Jonathan Harrington, fifing all the way as he ran to join his father on the Green.

Standing at her open door, his mother, Abigail, listened proudly and fearfully. Two young women stood silently beside her, each with an arm around their mother's waist. Indoors, her eldest daughter sat at the table, comforting a child of her own.

Abigail said nothing. There never was need for words between her and her daughters. They knew one another perfectly. They knew what she was thinking as she listened to the drum and fife singing a freedom song on the Green.

He's there because I woke him. I could've let him sleep. He's only sixteen. I could've let him sleep. But something screamed inside of me, and made me end his dream: *"Jonathan, get up! The redcoats are coming!"* Did they need his fife? They've got the drum. Did they need his name? They've got nine Harringtons without him. But I waked him, I waked him.

"Mother," one of the girls said gently, "if you had let Jonathan sleep, he'd never have forgiven you."

Across from the Green, women and children were at every window, watching their men form ranks. Before the fife had sung out, fifty-seven Minute Men could be counted. Now, twenty more farmers rushed forward.

"Remember, men," Parker cried out, "don't fire unless fired on. But if they mean to have a war, let it begin here!"

While the farmers paraded, Pitcairn in his red coat was leading his six companies up the road.

Before he could see what lay ahead, the major began to hear the beat of the American drum, then the saucy tune of the fife.

He ordered the column to halt and addressed his troops. "I don't have to tell you there's danger ahead. An hour ago, according to Major Mitchell, they had five hundred.

"Of course, if it comes to a fight, you could give them a drubbing to remember. I know you'd like nothing better than to make them crawl. But you heard the governor's orders. If there's shooting, let the rebels start it. Once they start, they'll be sorry."

He waited until Smith came into sight with his column of grenadiers. "All right, men! Now, prime and load!" They moved forward in double-quick time, pouring onto the Green.

At this moment it became clear that the Americans were in an impossible position. How could they have compared themselves with those who stopped the redcoats at Salem's bridge? Only a hundred and fifty royal troops had been on that expedition. Salem was no farming village, but a big port city, with hundreds of her own Minute Men.

The Salem citizens—men and women—outnumbered the redcoats. And they could simply raise the drawbridge and so keep Gage's men from the munitions he was after.

What could seventy-seven Lexington farmers do against eight hundred of the King's best troops? What sense was there in even trying? Wasn't it enough for Lexington to have sheltered Adams and Hancock, warned and guarded them?

Still, no one asked. The answer would've been too plain; numbers don't matter, bridges don't matter. All that matters is to be counted—to let Gage know we aren't sleeping, aren't hiding, aren't bowing to his fist.

For a moment, while the British advanced across the Green, a few of the farmers, a very few, drew back. But Captain Parker cried out, "Stand your ground!"

The advancing troops were amazed and relieved by what they saw. Some burst out laughing. "Where's their five hundred? Where's one hundred? Look at them. Not a uniform! They don't even hold their guns right. And *what* guns!"

Major Mitchell turned red. He'd been taken in by Revere's story. "Maybe the rest of them are waiting in ambush," he said.

At a hundred and fifty feet, the soldiers came to a smart halt. Pitcairn and two officers galloped toward the farmers.

The men didn't budge. "Let the troops pass by," Parker commanded, in a low tone. "Don't molest them unless they begin first. We're here. We're armed. Our wives see us, our children see us, and *they* see us. That's all we want."

Pitcairn had expected the ridiculous-looking band to melt away before him. But they stood like statues, muskets ready. He stopped his horse, and looked down at them.

It might be wiser simply to lead his companies past and hurry on to the bridges at Concord. But then, the news would spread—Adams would see to that. Eighty farmers daring to go on drilling, to bear arms in spite of the King's command—and the King's troops afraid to do anything about it!

"Disperse, you rebels, disperse!" Major Pitcairn shouted. "Lay down your arms!" His army watched, restless, eager for the signal. "Why don't you lay down your arms?"

From somewhere behind him, a shot rang out. Instantly, the redcoats fired a volley. Still, the Americans refused to budge.

John Munroe, seeing no one fall, said to his younger brother, "Have no fear, Ebenezer; it was a bluff. They fired blanks."

Once more the British took aim.

"They've fired something besides blanks now," Ebenezer replied, "for I am wounded."

First John, then his brother, discharged their guns into the main body of the enemy. Again, Ebenezer was hit—one bullet passed through his shirt, between his arm and body. The bullets flew so thick, he thought there was no chance of escape. He might as well fire his gun as stand still and do nothing.

One of the Harringtons was posted across from his own house. His wife and son watched from a window. Suddenly, he sank to the ground. Turning his face toward the window, he nodded to them and started up.

He stretched out his hands toward the window, as if begging for help, and fell again. Gathering his last strength, he rose on his hands and knees, and crawled slowly toward the house. His wife ran to meet him at the door, bent down, and put her arms around him. He was dead.

Captain Parker saw his men falling on all sides. The British were now rushing upon his little company from left and right. Once surrounded, it would be easy to kill or capture the whole lot of them. Parker ordered the company off the Green. Some turned as they ran, and fired back at their pursuers.

One man refused to obey the order. He was Jonas Parker, the captain's own cousin. Jonas had told his next-door neighbor, Reverend Clark, that no matter what others might do, he would never run from the enemy.

After the first fire of the redcoats, Jonas had loaded his musket calmly. He placed his hat, filled with ammunition, on the ground between his feet,

ready for the second charge. At the second fire
from the enemy, he was wounded, and sank to
his knees. But again he discharged his gun.

Now Jonas was the only American left on the
Green—except for the dead. On his knees, dying,
straining to load once more, he was pinned to the
earth by a bayonet.

The British had broken ranks and were rushing
after the Minute Men, with pistols blazing. Even
if Pitcairn had tried to order a halt, no one would
have heard him above the wild roar of the troops.

John Tidd had turned while fleeing. Horror-
stricken by the sight of Jonas Parker's death, he'd
forgotten to save himself. A British officer on
horseback rushed upon him and struck him down
with his sword.

The troops were slowly formed into ranks again.
The Americans had got enough of a beating to
keep their distance from now on.

Surveying the dead on the grass, looking from
window to window at the faces of women and
children, Pitcairn couldn't share the exultation of
his men. "Bad . . . bad . . ." he mumbled, "I told
them not to fire first. . . .

"Who was it anyway? Could it have been—
could we *say* it was—one of the rebels? From behind that stone wall maybe? Or the upper window of that Meeting House? That's it! Of course!

Nobody can say I didn't try. 'Disperse!' I begged them. The fools!"

Hearing the guns, Smith had spurred his horse forward. He listened to Major Pitcairn's report. What had happened was not part of Gage's plan. Come to think of it, what had happened was exactly the sort of thing he had been trying to avoid. Yet, as Pitcairn said, the rebels had started it, and the King's troops were obliged to end it.

They *had* ended it, and well. The victory was complete. Before them, the road to Concord was open. They fired a volley and gave three cheers —three thunderous cheers—so the towns round about could think it over.

Where were the rebels now? Dispersed, hiding behind walls! Or dead, on the grass.

What loss had the King's troops suffered? Pitcairn's horse and a sergeant.

And the saucy fife, with its tune that had frightened them so from a distance? Silent!

Heads high, the eight hundred took up their line of march for Concord.

## DAY OF GLORY: *Six A.M.*

*T*he fife was silent. Nothing moved on the ground; no sound moved in the air—except the stamp of British boots, in perfect rhythm, moving quickly out of sight and out of hearing.

Slowly the sun stuck out its head from the hills. It looked down at the Green in wonder. Never had there been such a stillness.

But wait! A boy was running, as fast as his legs could carry him. It was Abijah Harrington, thirteen years old. The fife song of his cousin Jona-

than, and the drumbeat of his friend, William, had
roused him just before the battle. Daniel and
Thaddeus, his grown-up brothers, were both on
the Green. So was his brother-in-law, Samuel. It
had required all of Mrs. Harrington's strength to
keep her youngest at home.

"But I must see the redcoats!" he pleaded. "I
won't go near. Just a glimpse of them, Mother!"

Now the shooting was over. She heard the three
cheers of the British, then the silence. It was last-
ing too long, this silence. She thought unbearable
thoughts about her sons—yet she hadn't the courage to drag herself out to the Green. Let Abijah
find out what there was to find out! His eyes were
afraid of nothing, his heart would not easily be
hurt. So she stood away from the door, and let
him go.

His heart thumped much faster than William's
drum, as he neared the road. "I must, I must see
the redcoats!" But the British were gone. He raced
across the Green to see if he could pick up a
souvenir of the enemy.

The tender, young, April grass had been easily
crushed beneath the soldiers' boots. He could trace
their line of march. But what was here? A red
pool! A pool of blood that was already soaking
into the earth! He'd found a souvenir after all!

As he ran back toward the Meeting House, he
saw groups of women and children. Just as he

prepared to shout the news of British blood, he suddenly realized that no sound at all was coming from the people—that they were simply bending toward the ground.

Then the thought seized him, and he stopped in his tracks. *Dead . . . we have dead . . .* Not Daniel! Not Thaddeus! Not Jonathan! Not any of the Jonathans! He hurried to the nearest group.

Now, from behind bushes and stone fences, the Minute Men returned. Ashen-faced, the rifles useless on their shoulders, they appeared. One by one, they returned to the Green, hoping it would look as trim and lovely as yesterday. Hoping the fallen would rise and greet them. But they knew it would never again look the same, nor would they themselves ever be the same.

Though Thomas Hadley was an old man, though the cold night outdoors without sleep had done him no good, he came back first. There was something he had to know. While the bullets flew, trying not to lose sight of his three sons, he'd caught a glimpse of something which he refused to believe. The spot would not be hard to find. He came around the Meeting House, and could walk no farther.

There they stood, as he knew they would be standing: Ebenezer and Benjamin, the two who hadn't been hit, clinging to their mother. And their sister-in-law, Betty, on her knees, smoothing back her dead husband's hair.

"Samuel, my son," the old man sobbed.

Down from the hill and across the swamp came the brothers, Ebenezer and John Munroe. They'd seen nothing but the British. They had discharged their guns into the smoke-covered ranks and fled, forgetting even to look for their father. Hadn't he made a name for himself in the French and Indian Wars, serving again four years later?

Despite his sixty years Robert Munroe could still use a rifle as well as any of them. It wasn't for nothing the company had chosen him as ensign. The boys were sure their father could take care of himself, and of a few redcoats, too. But they hadn't realized that a good ensign is one of the last to retreat. The British had been out to get the leaders first, and Munroe was not hard to find.

Now, John and Ebenezer came down from the hill and across the swamp. Close to the Green they found the silent group that was waiting for them. Their wives hurried to meet them, so they'd not have to take the final steps alone. Both sisters were there, too. The boys glanced down at their father's body; then, silently, circled their mother's waist. It was only then that tears started, and she bit her lip to stop the quivering.

Robert Munroe's wife had sat through the

night, knitting. She had sat alone, and listened to the drums, then the fife, then the guns, then the silence. After the silence had lasted a long while, she'd put away the knitting and gone down to the Green.

There she'd found her husband. One by one her married daughters had come, from their own homes, so that now she was no longer alone. And here was Lydia, hurrying to find out how it was with her own son. Ah! you see me, sister. Come, take my hand! I, too, am a widow, now.

Suddenly, a young boy's voice rang through the stillness. *"Redcoats! Six of them!"* It was Abijah. Not satisfied with the souvenir of British blood, he'd gone hunting for more. Something red had moved through the woods, off the road. Tiptoeing close, he'd discovered six redcoats, pointing and whispering.

This news electrified the village. Twenty men broke away from their families. They surrounded the redcoats and overpowered them without firing a single shot. The prisoners refused to say why they'd stayed on in the village. Was it to look for Adams and Hancock? Was it to plunder from the houses of those who stood mourning on the Green?

"We fell behind and lost our way," they mumbled. Guards were appointed to take them

to Adams at Woburn. Lexington had its dead; now
they had prisoners as well.

The wounded were rushed to nearby homes.
Two were carried to the Clark house, for Lucy
Clark and the Boston ladies to take care of. One
of these was Prince Estabrook. Of all the fighters
that morning, he alone had no one rushing to
greet and praise him. Prince was a Negro slave,
owned by the Estabrook family. Knowing more
than any of the others how it was not to be free,
he'd begged to join Parker's company. All night
he'd waited with the others. And at daybreak he
was among those who met the enemy face to
face.

For Prince and his wounded companion, the
parson had words of strength and comfort. Then
he put on his cloak. "I must speak to the people.
And yet," he sighed, "after so many years of
preaching, I'm afraid the words will be wrong."

A crowd was assembled before the Meeting
House. The dead lay side by side. The survivors
stood guard around them, and the women and
children formed a huge circle around the men.
Little Abijah's news about the six redcoats had
drawn them out of their separate circles. Now all
were acquainted, deeply acquainted, with each
other's sorrows—they had become one.

It was time for the words, the right words, to be
spoken. As soon as Clark appeared, the crowd

parted for him. He stood before each of the dead
in turn. When he saw the face of John Brown, he
wept—in front of all his congregation.

Seven days ago—the sun just a little higher
than now—he'd passed the field where John and
his father were plowing. "Good morning, Reverend!" the young man had called out. "You must
wish me a happy birthday."

"Happy birthday, indeed! And how old are you?
Let me guess. You were just learning your prayers
by heart when I first mounted the pulpit, here in
Lexington. That was almost twenty years ago. Are
you twenty-five?"

"Wrong!" John had laughed in his hearty way.
"I'm twenty-four."

"Time to get married."

The boy had blushed. "Not a bad idea."

But old Daniel, halting his work, had shaken
his finger at the parson. "Now don't you be putting ideas into Johnny's head! Remember, he's
the only boy I have left. Do you want to leave a
man of seventy all alone, with such fields to plow?"

For each of the dead, Jonas Clark had a hundred memories. But now was not the time. Looking up into the sun, he prayed quietly, then
spoke, at first slowly, softly, but soon in a voice
that drove the echo of the British cheers out of
Lexington forever.

"God, you witnessed today the deed of your

sons—and you saw what was done to them. I ask: were you surprised to see them standing before their Meeting House with guns? Were you surprised to see them put aside all thought of comfort, and life itself, for the sake of their town's honor, for the sake of their families' freedom?

"Knowing them so well, you must know why they did it. Not because I, or Samuel Adams, or anyone else, bade them do it, but because it was not in them to do otherwise.

"We, too, assembled here, knew them well. They were needed, greatly needed, and greatly loved. Without them, our fields will be empty, and our hearts . . . But our grief and our pride will not be lonely. Already, the news travels on the wings of the four winds, beyond time and place. A million hands will be placed on our shoulders, begging a share of this grief, a share of this pride."

For a moment, he was silent, searching from face to face. Then he continued. "Often, you have heard me say that a life well-lived is never ended. This morning I say it more surely than ever before. Though their faces be lost to the sun, *these men are living!* They live now, and will live as long as freedom is cherished!"

His voice rang out: "To their murderers I say: The battle you began this morning is not ended, nor will you be the ones to end it. Before this sun reaches the opposite hill, it will see much. The road from Boston to Concord goes both ways, and you must pass through Lexington once more before you get home. Our rusty guns were laughable to you, but out of their mouths will leap a song such as the world has never known.

"Oh God, give us the might to do your work this day! An eye for an eye! A tooth for a tooth!"

Trembling, he stepped forward into the crowd.

## DAY OF GLORY: *Seven A.M.*

*I*t was true, what the parson said about the traveling of the news. Even as he spoke, men on horseback were rushing across New England.

As soon as his wounded arm was washed and covered, young Ebenezer Munroe had jumped on his horse and galloped into the morning without a good-by. Wherever he saw people—at every cluster of houses—he slowed the horse long enough so that his cry would be understood: "To arms! To arms! The war has begun! Six farm-

ers murdered on Lexington Green!" (Eight were
dead—but he'd left before the full count was in.)

On and on he sped, through streets and fields
and woods and more streets, over bridges and
around hills—shouting till his lips were dry and
his throat ached, till the blood oozed through the
bandage, through the shirt.

Everywhere, while the echo—the terrible echo
of his words—still hung in the air, the people took
his task of alarming the countryside upon themselves. If there was a bell to ring out the alarm,
they rang it. If there was a cannon to boom out
the alarm, they fired it. Farmers left their plows
and rushed home to grab their muskets. Minute
Men hurried to the place of assembly. Others
went alone, taking the fastest road to Lexington.

And still young Ebenezer Munroe galloped on,
into the face of the sun, until he became dizzy
from lack of blood. When he couldn't quite finish
the words he was gasping out, a man ran out,
took the reins from his hand, and gently lifted
him down.

Meanwhile, other messengers were flying along
other roads, alarming the people wherever they
went. One rode toward Worcester—more than
thirty miles away. Three headed in the other direction, for Boston. One was instructed not to stop
until he reached Warren's house, while the other

two warned patriot leaders in Cambridge and Brookline.

One raced toward Concord, galloping cross-country. But even before he got there, that village had already been twice alarmed.

About two in the morning, Prescott had pounded on Colonel Barrett's door, and shouted so loud, that windows opened in all the nearby houses. "For God's sake, open!"

An old man doesn't like to lose his sleep, doesn't enjoy running downstairs and opening his door to the night wind. But when Barrett heard about the British officers on the road, all thoughts of sleep were forgotten.

"Dress warmly," Prescott warned. "It's a bitter cold night." But Barrett had no time to look for winter clothes that were already packed away. He assembled the Concord Committee of Safety, and military officers.

William Emerson, the young patriot parson, rang the bell of his church as a signal to the people that, for the rest of the night, they'd have more important business than dreaming. Then he took his gun, and reported.

Reuben Brown, one of Concord's best horsemen, was sent by back lanes toward Lexington, to spy out the enemy if he could.

Guards were stationed at both bridges, and in the center of the village. The main task was to remove as many of the cannon and other stores as possible. Colonel Barrett was in charge of the militia, but everyone agreed that removing the supplies was more important. Others could parade the men. No one but Barrett knew the whereabouts of all the military stores.

Ever since trouble with England had begun to come to a head, Barrett had been in charge of the manufacture and collection of guns and ammunition. Some of the munitions were already in safe hands far from Concord. Revere had brought orders to do that, last Sunday. But much was hidden here.

Without any delay, the colonel and his staff rolled up their sleeves and got to work. From the minute the conference was over, until the redcoats could be seen on the road, there was no letup. Four cannon were carried to nearby Stow, six others to the outlying farms. Powder, bullets, cannon balls, were heaped onto wagons and sent to Acton.

Other supplies were hidden, with the help of women and children, in private buildings and in the woods. While they worked, the darkness slowly lifted, and the night was over.

As the first rays of light began to push up into the eastern sky, the Minute Men paraded on the Common. Then they stood around, uncertainly. The night had gone and the British had not come.

Like the men of Lexington, they weren't sure the enemy *was* coming. The captain dismissed them with instructions to gather again at the beat of the drum.

They had scarcely dispersed when, once more, the drum beat to arms. Ninety men marched down below the village, in full view of the Lexington road.

About the same time, some of the Minute Men from nearby Lincoln came into town and paraded with the Concord militia. They'd been the first to hear of the fighting at Lexington, and had rushed furiously to reach Concord ahead of the British.

It was seven o'clock, by Major Buttrick's watch, when the redcoats came into view. Eight hundred men, in rich red uniforms, with every button, every medal, every pistol blazing like a sun; eight hundred men, marching in perfect rhythm!

To the watchers on the hillside, this army appeared to be a monstrous red serpent, moving hungrily forward to snap up the village.

Reverend Emerson stood in the forefront of the line. For ten years he had preached sermons about liberty; but it was not enough to fire others with the love of freedom. If he was truly the shepherd of this flock, then he must shield them on this day of days, not with words alone, but with his very body.

Around him, now, were about one hundred and fifty men. Some, he could see, were tense and frightened by the blaze of the redcoat medals. "Are we less than the men of Lexington? Let us stand our ground!" Emerson shouted. "If we die, let us die here!"

The men were divided. Compared to the enemy, they were only a handful. "Let us go and meet them!" someone cried.

Eleazar Brooks, of Lincoln, shook his head. "No —it will not do for *us* to begin the war."

The British were moving quickly. There was hardly any time for talking things over. Some agreed with Reverend Emerson that they should stand their ground and resist the enemy. But a greater number felt otherwise.

Colonel Barrett raised his arms for silence. The decision, the responsibility, must be his. "We'll retire over North Bridge and assemble on the burying-ground hill. There we can watch the movements of the enemy without being seen, and wait for reinforcements."

They stayed until the shadows of the redcoats were almost upon them, then turned and marched away. Reverend Emerson, the last to leave, looked back once at the handsome young killers, and murmured, "We shall meet again."

## DAY OF GLORY: *Eight A.M.*

*T*wo hours after leaving his home, the rider from Lexington galloped down Hanover Street toward Joseph Warren's house. At the sound of the hoofs, Boston John picked up his musket and opened the shutter to see who was coming with such speed.

Quickly he unlocked the door, and let the exhausted lad in. "Shh!" he whispered. "The doctor's been up most of the night. He's just now really gotten to sleep. What is it?"

"I'm from Lexington," the boy gasped. "Must see Dr. Warren right away!"

"Is it very important? Can't it wait until the doctor wakes?"

"Adams sent word—the doctor must be told at once—six of our men were killed by the British on Lexington Green this morning."

The servant stepped back in horror. "*Six killed!* Then they've started it. Stay down here and keep an eye on the street. I'll go up and wake him."

Boston John opened the door. "Doctor!" he called, softly.

No sound came from the bed but a deep, regular breathing. Warren's face was troubled and both fists were pressed against his ears as though to defend them from a terrifying sound.

"Dr. Warren!" John repeated.

The third time his name was called, Warren opened his eyes. The sun blinded him. He sat up wildly. "What time is it?"

"A few minutes after eight."

"After *eight*?" The doctor looked around the room as though it were a crime for him to be in it. "How'd you let me sleep so late? I asked you to wake me early today."

"I just didn't have the heart to. I wouldn't have awoken you now, either, except that there's a

messenger from Lexington downstairs. Mr. Adams
sent him."

"That means Adams is safe. Thank God!"
Joseph Warren dressed hurriedly, and ran down
the stairs two at a time, buttoning his shirtsleeves
as he went. "My name's Warren. You have a message for me?"

The lad nodded, and repeated what he'd told
Boston John.

"*Six killed?*" Warren gasped. "*Six of our men?*"

The messenger reconstructed the whole scene,
from the beating of the Lexington drum to the
three British cheers. He'd brought the news to
Adams and Hancock, safe at Woburn. Adams
had sent him on to Boston.

As he listened, Warren began to feel a throb-
bing in his throat. The drum had beaten after all,
the fife had sung. The farmers had come out; had
paraded before the enemy. They had not dispersed when they were commanded to; had not
put down their arms. They had fired back at the
King's troops.

Oh, glory! glory! Eighty men—not soldiers,
really, but plain farmers—who'd had maybe a
month's training, an hour a day!

*Cheered* had they, those redcoated fools? Let
them, let them enjoy their three precious cheers.
How could they be expected to know the mean-

ing of twenty minutes on Lexington Green? Even
to America, the full meaning will not come all at
once. But it will unfold, for them and for us, oh
yes! while the hours of this day unfold.

Boston John was frightened by the look on Warren's face. "You're sick!" he cried and put his hand
on the young man's forehead. "Hot as an oven.
I knew it!"

But Warren waved the hand away. "Sick? I've
never felt stronger in my life." He walked back
and forth. "This is the day! All our years have
flowed into this one day, and all the years to
come will flow out of it. . . . But what am I
doing here, talking? Boston John—please help me!
I must be on the next ferry to Charlestown.
There's much to be settled, and no time at all to
do it properly."

"Of course, Doctor," the servant nodded. "Tell
me what you need. But I can't let you go without food."

"There's no time. Fetch Will Eustis. If he's still
asleep, drag him here in his night clothes. Meanwhile, there are notes to write."

The messenger was returning to Lexington. At
the door, Warren said: "Thank you for bringing
the news so quickly! Tell your people—" In spite
of himself, the tears came to his eyes and he had
to turn away. "What words are there . . . ?"

Clenching his fists, he turned to the messenger again. "Tell your people I'll be there soon," he said.

Now he was alone in the house. He went to a closet, unlocked a hidden chest, and took from it a bright, new rifle. As he turned, he happened to see his reflection in the mirror, and was forced to smile.

Joseph Warren—soldier! Just look at me: Powdered, gentlemanly wig; gentlemanly doctor's suit; gentlemanly white hands—but in the hands— a gun! He sat down at the desk, found two sheets of paper, and wrote.

DEAR MOTHER—If you know, by the time this note reaches you, what happened at Lexington this morning, you will not have to be told where I am. I remember your warnings in recent days: that I should keep my life in safety. But neither can I forget what you taught me and my brothers even when we were infants. . . .

If my love for America and my desire for her freedom are too great, it is you who are to blame. If it should chance that we never meet again, know that my heart is now, as always, full of pride and love. I thank you for making me a man and a patriot. You will do as well for my children, too. With devotion, JOSEPH.

For a moment he had to put down the pen.

Words had always come easily to him—but the next letter was hard to get down on paper.

My beloved children—Once again I must disappoint you. I will not be able to see you this evening, as we had all hoped. There is a sudden operation to be performed in the countryside; you would be ashamed of your father if he did not go. Keep well, my darlings; let us do things that will make us proud of one another. Your ever-loving father.

Will Eustis came in.

"Well, Dr. Eustis," (Warren had never called him that before) "it's come. I'm crossing over to Charlestown by the next ferry. When—if ever— we meet again, is an open question."

"Please don't talk that way, Doctor!"

"Why not? The plain fact is that I expect to be as close to bullets as possible, as soon as possible, and as long as possible."

Eustis looked down. It would be senseless to plead.

Warren folded his letters as he spoke. "I've been pleased these last months, Will, with the skill and good sense you've shown. You can't imagine how good a doctor feels when he knows his patients are being left in safe hands. . . . From my daybook you'll see who should be visited today, and what treatment they should have." He handed his student the book, and smiled; then rose from behind the desk and held out his hand. A glance at the clock had alarmed him. Each ferry might be the last. He picked up the rifle.

Boston John had been silent at the door. The grim sound of his master's voice, and the talk of bullets, had worried him. Now he caught sight of the gun.

"What are you doing with that gun?"

"What's wrong with it? It's a good one."

"But . . . you wouldn't even know how to use it. . . . You're just going out there and get killed. I know it!"

Warren put his arm around the troubled man. "That's not so. I can shoot pretty well. Where do you think I've been running off to every morning this month? I've been drilling. Did you think I was just looking out at the empty harbor?"

John broke away and ran toward the kitchen. "Wait! I've got *my* gun in there. If you take the ferry, *I* take the ferry! If anybody aims at your head, I aim at his head!"

Warren stopped him. "No, not yet. Maybe later. There's work to be done here. The Committee needs help. And John, these notes I've scribbled to my mother and children, will you deliver them, please? And without that nonsense? No sobbing, no moaning! You're the one who's got to cheer them up!"

Warren's horse stood ready. He mounted and started off.

## DAY OF GLORY: *Nine A.M.*

*J*ust twelve hours ago, the Common of Boston had swarmed with whispering redcoats. Now, in the bright rays of the sun, a new swarm prepared to move out of the city. This time, in the broad daylight, nothing could be concealed. Anyone with time and patience could stand across from the grass, and count one thousand troops. Any schoolboy could point out Lord Percy galloping from company to company, lining up the troops under his command.

It was known to everyone that Percy planned to join Smith. But a full hour had passed since troops were formed into lines, looking fit and eager for a big day's work. An hour and a half had passed since Gage's courier had brought Percy the order. What was taking so long?

The governor had slept till a little after seven. There was a faint smile around his lips when the servant entered to wake him.

"Your Excellency, a messenger from Colonel Smith is downstairs. He *says* he's been knocking for almost an hour, but neither I nor any of the other servants heard him. Perhaps he was knocking at a tavern door on the way."

"Help me into my robe!" Gage commanded. He hurried to the top of the stairs, and shouted impatiently: "Come up, come up, don't stand there! Give me the paper!"

The messenger climbed the stairs, murmuring, "Colonel Smith told me to waste no time. I knocked for almost an hour. Look at my knuckles!"

Gage snatched the paper. His face reddened. He crumpled it into a tiny ball, and threw it with all his strength into the messenger's face. "Is this the Colonel's idea of a joke?" he screamed.

The lad looked down and turned to go. His cheek hurt, where the paper had struck. His knuckles were bleeding from endless knocking, but it would not do to say anything.

"Wait! wait a minute! Show me that thing!" Gage smoothed the note, read it over and over. *The report is that 500 farmers are massing at Lexington. Send Percy with reinforcements.* What time did Smith write it? Where was his army then?

The answers didn't help. Finally, Gage began shouting orders. Instantly, Province House became alive. Doors creaked open and slammed shut. Servants, couriers, officers rushed about, knocking against each other in their haste to obey the governor's commands.

In his robe and slippers, Gage paced back and forth—nervously clasping his hands together, tugging at his wig, mumbling to himself: this is the end, the end, the end.

Secretary Flucker rushed upstairs. There were times when his flattery and nodding helped the nerves. But not this morning!

"I don't want bloodshed!" Gage kept saying. "At least—I mustn't be responsible for it. What's the time? Seven-thirty? Smith should be done with Concord by now, and ready to start back. Do you think he has the brains to bypass Lexington and get to Concord without meeting the rebels face to face?"

Flucker nodded, as he always did to be on the safe side. "Well . . . you told him."

Gage shook his head. "But I know the men. They've been cooped up far too long."

It was then that Percy had burst in. "The courier told me, Governor. Give me the orders, and I'll set out."

Since then an hour and a half had gone by. In no time at all, Percy had assembled his thousand men. After a good night's sleep, they were wide awake and hungry for action. Five hundred rebels didn't scare them.

Lord Percy would have marched out long before, if not for Major Pitcairn. Where the devil was that rascal anyway? Since the marines were going to be an important section of Percy's force, an order had been sent for the major to march with his men. The couriers were still looking for Pitcairn, when a rider came galloping onto the Common with a message from the governor.

"Good news! There were no hundreds in the way at Lexington—only a handful of farmers, without one proper gun among them. Major Pitcairn dispersed them at daybreak—not a single loss to our troops— then on to the bridges at Concord. Nevertheless, I want you to go up and meet him. On your way, the countryside will be watching closely. See that the men look and act their best! Don't spare the fifes and drums! Give the rebels a show they'll remember!

Percy laughed aloud, and called over his officers
to share the joke. "Only a handful. Shouldn't we
have known it? And Pitcairn, of course! Why
hadn't anyone remembered? Why hadn't Gage
reminded us that Pitcairn was already on the
scene?"

An hour lost. Still, it hardly mattered. "We'll
give them a fifing and drumming all right! We'll
Yankee Doodle them into the ground!"

Percy gave the order to march. First came the
band, playing Yankee Doodle as impudently as possible. Then the splendid troops, followed by a
baggage train, and two cannon—just to make the
show complete. Slowly the army moved off the
Common, down Tremont Street, and through the
town gate.

As they pushed through Roxbury, some of the
soldiers entertained themselves by shouting insults at the people. Percy ordered a halt to such
behavior. The men must look straight ahead, chin
up, as though the citizens of Roxbury were beneath notice.

All at once, Lord Percy became conscious of a
hated melody being chirped up at him from the
roadside. Looking down he saw a schoolboy of
nine or ten, skipping along beside him. The lad
was smiling wickedly up at Percy's face as he
sang verses of the ballad of "Chevy Chase" in his
high, small voice:

*" 'Tell me who ye are,' he says,*
*'Or whose men that ye be;*
*Who gave you leave to hunt in this chase*
*In the spite of me?'*
*"The first man that ever him answer made,*
*It was the good Lord Percy . . ."*

Percy knew very well that the famous old ballad ended with that other Percy's death. He had a
good mind to halt the march and give the saucy
lad a beating. Imagine! Even the young, shouting
treason!

But it would be more sensible to pretend that
he hadn't heard the singing—keep riding, look
straight ahead. In a few minutes the boy would
be far behind. Who could tell what glories this
day might bring to the name of Percy? Perhaps
new stanzas would some day be written to that
old melody.

What a stubborn little fellow, though! Weren't
his legs ever going to give out? And that voice
—how could one help but hear it, above all the
instruments in the band:

*"Of fifteen hundred archers of England,*
*Went away but fifty and three . . ."*

Without realizing what he was doing, Percy

spurred the horse savagely. The schoolboy was outdistanced. Yet there was a ringing in the ears of the British commander.

## DAY OF GLORY: *Ten A.M.*

$S$oon after daybreak, a rider had passed through Acton. Forty of that village were Minute Men. Twice a week, since November, Captain Davis had drilled his men, and drilled them well. Being a gunsmith himself, Davis had seen to it that his company, at least, was properly armed.

From house to house the horseman had galloped, until the entire village was alarmed. As soon as they heard that redcoats were on their way to Concord, the men dressed, kissed their

117

families good-by and hurried to the captain's house.

Deacon Hosmer's son, Abner, had been the first to arrive. With him had come the fifer of the company, Luther Blanchard. When Luther was a little boy, during the French and Indian Wars, his father had died in battle. Now he lived with the Hosmers and was learning the mason's trade.

Right behind these two had come James Hayward, supplied with a pound of powder and forty balls. If James had decided to stay at home that morning, no one could've been angry. Part of his left foot had been cut off by an ax when he was a child, so that he was not really fit for military duty.

But this young schoolteacher wouldn't let a couple of toes, more or less, make any difference. "I've taught the children of Acton that freedom is worth dying for," he'd told his father. "Could I ever dare to meet one of them on the road afterwards, if I stayed at home today?"

A half dozen more had crowded into the kitchen before Captain Davis appeared, heavyhearted. What a time to be leaving Hannah alone! All four children were sick—from the baby to the eldest.

The sun was over an hour old, and it was decided not to delay any longer. "The British won't wait—neither can we. Those who leave home too

late to meet us on the road, can find their way to
Concord alone."

James Hayward ran over to the grindstone.

"We're leaving, Jim. What are you up to?"

"I'll be just a minute." He bent toward the stone,
and started grinding the point of the bayonet. "I
expect before night we shall come to a push with
them, and I want my bayonet sharp."

Hannah followed her husband to the door. In
front of all these people she couldn't expect that
he would take her into his arms. He turned
around once, as though there were something he
wanted to tell her. But all he said was, "Take
good care of the children."

She nodded. In a few minutes he was out of
sight.

With Barker drumming and Blanchard fifing,
the Acton Company set out along Strawberry
Hill Road. When they were quite close to the
Concord boundary, Davis pointed to Barrett's
house and mill. Both buildings swarmed with redcoats in search of hidden stores.

"We'll cut through the fields. And—no music,
please, till we're out of earshot."

Some of the men were disappointed. They
weren't afraid of being seen by the enemy, and
would have been willing to answer a volley right
then and there. Luther wanted the redcoats to
hear him play "White Cockade!"

But at Captain Davis' command, the Acton men swung off the road and marched across fields in a straight course. Halfway across the field, the drum and fife took up their song.

At the sound, a window in Widow Brown's tavern opened. Inside, four redcoats had finished searching for bullets and powder, everywhere but under Mrs. Brown's apron. Now they were drinking more than they should—to make up for all the hours they'd been marching without a drop to drink.

The redcoated soldiers sprawled out, as though they'd like to spend the rest of the day in those chairs. Thirteen-year-old Charles Handley had been observing them through the keyhole, but when he heard the music of the Acton men, he ran to the window.

How tiny the Company seemed, in the midst of the huge green fields! But the drum and fife made quite a noise—especially the fife. That man really knew how! What was he playing? "White Cockade?" That's it!

They were quite close now—marching very fast in time to the music. He waved. All at once, the Acton men veered east and disappeared down the back road to North Bridge.

When he couldn't hear the notes of the rebel song any more, the boy shut the window and went back to his position at the keyhole. He'd never seen a redcoat before, except in pictures. Here were *four* of them, sitting at exactly the same table where he'd eaten his breakfast an hour ago!

On the burying hill overlooking North Bridge, four hundred Americans were assembled. They'd been streaming in from near and far: Carlisle, Chelmsford, Westford, Littleton. When the Acton Company marched into view, a cheer went up. The company marched in perfect rhythm onto the hill and took a position at the left of the Concord men.

Several fires had been set by the redcoats, and Major Buttrick had called the leaders together to decide what should be done. Davis joined them.

"Of course," a man from Littleton argued, "we must cross the bridge without delay."

"Yes, but how?" another asked. "The only way we can reach the bridge is by that causeway— and it's so narrow, only two at a time can march through. Our men would be mowed down."

Reverend Emerson was impatient. "There are over four hundred of us, and less than a hundred of them stationed at the bridge."

"True, the advantage in number is momentarily on our side. But compare our weapons with theirs. Why, they can load and fire three times to our once."

"We've got more than Lexington had," Emerson replied.

"Yes, and they'll give us more than they gave Lexington. If we do get past the hundred at the bridge, which I doubt, Smith will be waiting for us with six hundred more! Do you know what Abijah Pierce has to fight with? And he's the Colonel of Lincoln's Minute Company, mind you. He's armed with a cane! And his whole company has one French War bayonet among them."

"If Pierce is willing to march with a cane, those with muskets can offer to do no less."

Major Buttrick had been silent, allowing the others to speak themselves out. Now he spoke quietly. "We'll force the bridge. The Minute Companies will have to lead the way. The enemy may decide to drive us back with bayonets, instead of firing, and only the Minute Men have bayonets."

Some nodded in agreement. Others were silent. Then Buttrick continued. "We know what dangers will be faced by the company in the lead. We also know what honors will come to it. Inasmuch as their own village is at stake, Concord will lead the way."

One of the Concord's captains looked down at the causeway, then up at his men. "I'd rather not, Major. My men are improperly armed. It would be suicide."

Buttrick reddened with anger and shame. He

himself was a Concord man. He turned to Davis, of
Acton. "Are you afraid to go? Are there ten in
your company who won't quit their place?"

Without a word, Davis wheeled around, hurried
back to his townsmen, drew his sword, and
shouted, "There isn't one man in my company
that's afraid to go! March!!" he cried. Then, leading them out of line, he brought them up on the
right, at the head of the column.

At that instant, black smoke rose in the center
of Concord. Was the Courthouse afire? Was this
their revenge for having failed to capture Hancock and Adams?

As the ugly smoke towered toward the clouds,
Hosmer left the lines and ran to where the leaders were still consulting. "Will you let them burn
the town down while you talk?" he screamed.

The talking ended. Colonel Barrett gave orders
to march at once, but not to fire unless fired upon
by the King's troops.

With Major Buttrick beside him, Davis led his
company in double ranks down the causeway to
the river. The others followed close behind.
Luther struck up the tune of "White Cockade."
This time, the redcoats could hear every saucy
twist of the tune.

Most of the enemy guard were entrenched on
the west side of the river, facing the hill. One
of the redcoat companies paraded smartly at the

bridge. Now that they saw the Minute Men approaching, they quickly recrossed the bridge and began to take up the planks.

"Let our bridge be!" Buttrick shouted, and ordered his men to go faster.

The Acton men ran toward the bridge. Seeing this, the enemy forgot about the planks, and joined ranks for battle.

When the Americans were a few rods away, the British opened fire. The first ball struck the water. Two or three shots followed, doing no damage.

"Is it bullets they're firing?" Davis asked.

Suddenly the firing stopped. "Yes," replied Luther, who was bleeding.

A volley hit them. Captain Davis fell dead. Another bullet struck Abner. He, too, died instantly. Ezekiel Davis, the blood gushing from his forehead, knelt sobbing beside his brother's body. Luther forgetting his own wound, bent above the teacher who had given his last lesson.

"Fire!" Buttrick cried. "For God's sake, fire!"

There was no holding back now. Swiftly the Acton men took aim and fired. One, no, two, no, three redcoats crumpled to the ground! Others clutched at wounds.

The British fell back, astonished by the taste of death. The guns they'd poked fun at had turned out to be not at all funny. Breaking ranks, they fell back toward the village, to the protection of the main body of troops, leaving behind their dead and wounded.

Watching them, the Americans were also astonished. Their own rugged hands, their very own muskets, were pushing back those whose march—until this moment—had always been forward. Forward against the Spanish, the Dutch, the French—forward through Canada, India, Africa—forward, over all the continents and waters of the earth. . . .

Colonel Abijah Pierce of Lincoln hurled his cane into the river. He tore from the hands of a wounded redcoat a bright new rifle. He looked back and smiled, showing off his treasure. "The war has begun," he said, "and this will be more than a souvenir!"

## DAY OF GLORY: *Eleven A.M.*

*P*ercy and his army had left Roxbury far behind. The band played loudly. The troops, with their bright bayonets glittering in the sunlight, looked like a flowing river as they pushed toward Cambridge.

But all the splendor seemed wasted. Only the sky was a witness. The houses were all shut up. Not a trace could be found of a single citizen. Even a boy singing "Chevy Chase" would have been better than the tight-lipped silence of these

126

houses. The redcoat music echoed through the Charles River valley and was flung back to their ears.

Now they approached the Great Bridge over the Charles. Across the river sat Cambridge. Surrounded by rich green woodlands, it looked peaceful and inviting! If it were not for a few troublemakers like Adams and Hancock, he could enjoy riding here without supply wagons, without cannon. Just a man, alone, enjoying the fragrance of the April air.

He looked down just in time. *There was no Great Bridge*—nothing at all but the swollen currents of the stream, its ripples glittering like bayonet points.

"Halt!" he shouted, and took out the map Gage had given him. There it was, plain as day: *Great Bridge across the Charles into Cambridge.* Hadn't Gage known that there wasn't any bridge? How old was the map?

It was two days old. This was surely rebel mischief! Percy raised spyglasses and peered across. Sure enough—near the riverbank, in the underbrush, huge planks lay hidden. He called his officers together, and let them look through the glasses. "Find half a dozen good swimmers in your company—no, a dozen would be better—and send them across. We'll get the bridge up in no time. Mmmm. . . . Clever work! On the way back

I think we'll stop off there, and ask a few questions."

The bridge was easily put up again, and the troops hurried across to make up for the time they'd lost. They went through Cambridge swiftly —no point putting up a show for empty houses. Not even a dog could be seen on the streets.

Percy was disappointed. He'd hoped by this time to know whether the work at Concord had come off smoothly, and where he could expect to meet Smith. But there was no one to question along the road. It was a dead city, and he was glad to leave it behind.

As soon as the sound of hoofs and boots faded away, Cambridge came to life again. True, the young fighters had all gone, and their families were in hiding. But the old men had stayed. Behind every wall, every fence, the eyes of old men had followed Percy's army. These old men had taken down the planks and upset Lord Percy's timetable.

"What fools we were, to leave the planks so near!" one of them muttered, when he saw the bridge had been restored. "We should've burned them, or shoved them downstream."

But another said, "And make Percy so angry he'd burn down the village?"

"*Wait! Look at the bridge!*" Most of them had been watching spellbound while the great army went by. The marching column was gone, yet something remained on the other side of the river. Some wagons seemed to be having a hard time getting across. A few planks hadn't been found and the bridge was dangerous for a large, loaded wagon.

Then their work hadn't been wasted after all! Without a moment's delay, they sent a courier through the woods to Menotomy—the next village.

The old men of Menotomy were on guard behind walls and fences, all along the road. Percy's army had just now pushed through—and they still seemed dazed by the spectacle.

"News from Cambridge!" the courier shouted. They crowded around in surprise. All the news so far had been from Lexington and Concord. What could there be to tell about Cambridge?

"We took the Great Bridge down, and the redcoats put it up again. But the supply wagons couldn't get across as quickly as the troops. They'll probably be along in fifteen or twenty minutes."

This was news indeed! A dozen oldsters hurried into Cooper's tavern to talk it over.

"We can stop them! We've got the men and guns to do it!" cried David Lamson, who had good reason to hate the British. Lamson's mother was an

Indian woman. The British had wronged her people many times.

"We can stop them!" others agreed, clutching weapons as outworn as themselves.

But there were some who hesitated. "We're here to protect the women and children of Menotomy, not to make war."

"Not to make war?" shouted Samuel Whittemore, eighty-one years old. "They've started it already. In other towns, men may be dying this minute, for the sake of *our* women and children."

"Fine talk. But what's in those wagons? How many redcoats are protecting them? All they need is one small cannon, and they'll finish us off in no time."

Lamson was impatient. Time was running out. "We can stop them in front of the Meeting House, and shoot up their horses. Even if we lose, at least we'll hurt them, slow them down some more."

There was one last objector—"When Percy finds out, he'll burn down every house in Menotomy."

"Better to build new houses that we can be free in, than to live like slaves in the old ones!" Parson Payson stepped forward.

His words amazed them. Payson had preached patience and forgiveness so often that his congregation was beginning to call him a Tory—one of King George's men. But that was before the news from Lexington. Now there could be no patience, nor any talk of peace.

"Lamson is right!" the parson said. "It is our duty to keep away from the British whatever supplies they need. If some of us die or kill, let God judge who is to blame for this morning's work."

The consultation was over. It was agreed that Lamson should lead them.

Opposite the Meeting House stood a bank, a wall of earth and stone. Behind this they crouched, loaded their guns, and waited. It was not long before the wagons appeared.

"Take aim, men!" Lamson whispered. When the first horses were directly in front of them, he stood up. "Stop and surrender," he shouted, "or you are all dead men!"

Instead of obeying, the driver whipped his horses savagely ahead. A few of the sergeant's guard, curious about the noise, stuck their heads out of the wagon. One man laughed at the quaint old Indian. Here was an interesting spectacle! Since Roxbury, there'd been nothing to see but trees and empty houses.

"Fire!" Lawson commanded.

The old men discharged a volley. A few of the horses screamed and rolled over. Others ran wild, bleeding. The redcoat who had smiled at

the ridiculous old man was shot through the head.
He toppled down onto the road. Two or three of
the sergeant's guard cried out in pain. The others
jumped from the wagons and raced off into the
woods.

"After them, men!" cried Lamson, leading the
way. Reverend Payson, and a sixteen-year-old
boy were left in charge of the baggage. They
drew the abandoned wagons into a hollow,
dragged away the dead horses, and led the surviving ones into hiding. If Percy should turn
back to look for the missing supplies, he'd find no
trace.

The British ran blindly through the woods. The
Menotomy men, being much older, and slower
afoot, had trouble keeping up the chase. After
a while, some of them returned to the road, just
in time to capture a British officer, Lieutenant
Gould, who'd been sent from Concord to report
to Gage about the fight at North Bridge.

Meanwhile, six of the guards from the wagons
reached the shore of a huge pond. To keep their
rifles from falling into rebel hands, they threw
the guns into this pond. In a field an old woman
was digging dandelions. She seemed altogether
unaware of the events that were rocking America.

"Good day to you, Mother!" their leader said,
cheered by the sight of the old granny.

She looked up and nodded, looking them over one by one.

"We've been out walking," one of the guards said, "and seem to have lost our way. Can you show us a way back to Cambridge without going through the underbrush again?"

She stood up and smoothed her apron. "I'm a bit old to guide you myself, but my grandson will be glad to take you. He's over in that cottage by the water."

They thanked her. The spies had been right: plenty of loyal subjects could still be found in Massachusetts!

The old woman followed as they walked toward the cottage and knocked at the door. It opened, and out sprang a small company of armed men.

As the prisoners were marched away, she called after them in her high, trembly voice: "If you ever get back to England, don't forget to tell King George how six of his guards were captured by an old lady digging dandelions!"

The men of Menotomy roared with laughter, but the red-faced prisoners kept their mouths shut. Smoothing her apron again, she went slowly back into the field.

## DAY OF GLORY: *Noon*

*C*olonel Smith and Major Pitcairn sat on the lawn of one of Concord's taverns. They were sipping tea under the shade of a cherry tree while they watched the troops parading.

The reports Smith had received were excellent. South Bridge was in the hands of Captain Pole; North Bridge, guarded by Captain Laurie. Tories were showing the troops where important rebels might be found, and where supplies were hidden. A young British ensign, who had visited Concord a month before, was guiding three companies to Colonel Barrett's house and other hiding places of rebel guns.

Meanwhile, Pitcairn reported, the grenadiers and marines had done a good job in the center of the village. "We broke open about sixty barrels of powder. About five hundred pounds of balls lie at the bottom of the millpond and wells. I didn't try to stop the men when they cut down the Liberty Pole and burned it to ashes."

Somehow the Courthouse, where the words of treason still echoed, had been set afire, too. The two officers sipped tea slowly while the smoke lifted toward the clouds, until it, too, became a cloud—a black cloud for all Massachusetts to tremble at.

While the cup was still at Colonel Smith's lips, one of Captain Laurie's couriers came up, panting. "There's a great crowd of Americans on the hill across the river—right near North Bridge. They're forming into lines, and every minute more are joining."

Smith and Pitcairn winked at each other. "Like the five hundred at Lexington?" the major asked.

The same thought was in Smith's mind. Yet he slowly lifted his fat body out of the chair. "I'm taking no chances. You'll be in charge here, while I reinforce the bridge."

He marched his men slowly and was still far

from the bridge when the shooting began. Captain Laurie and his men came running back in wild disorder. From their gasping words, it was not easy to make out what had happened, except that the rebels had managed to push them back and to recapture the bridge.

Smith retreated to the center of town, to consider his next step. He was stunned by the news that Americans had dared to discharge a volley at the King's troops. And they were good marksmen, too, these farmers! Three British officers had been hit, including Lieutenant Gould.

After the lieutenant's wounded arm had been washed and dressed, Smith asked: "Do you feel strong enough for a long ride? I want you to take Gage a report of what's happened. I know I can depend on *you*. And, Lieutenant," he called, as the officer turned to go, "you'll surely meet Percy on the way. He's probably past Lexington by now. Tell him what's happened, and say we're waiting."

The second cup of tea, somehow, tasted flat. Smith raged against Captain Laurie. "Why didn't you let me know sooner how many of them were assembled? Why did you wait so long before pulling up the planks? Why didn't you let them cross over and then trap the whole lot of them?"

Captain Laurie needn't have bothered to answer. Smith wasn't really listening. It had happened—it was over—it was water under the bridge. *The bridge!*

Pitcairn worried about the British companies across the river, rounding up munitions.

"They'll get back all right," said Laurie. "The farmers were more shocked than we by what they'd done. They scattered as soon as it was over."

While Laurie was giving his report, Captain Pole with his hundred men marched up. They had become alarmed at the sound of shooting. They'd found a few guns and some powder, and had eaten enough to last them till Boston. Before returning, they'd removed all the planks of South Bridge.

"Yes—yes—" Smith said. "I'm sure you ate enough. I'll bet the women and children are laughing right now because of the tricks you let them play on you. An arsenal doesn't suddenly stop being an arsenal overnight. If I'd gone I wouldn't have returned with my stomach full and my hands empty."

Smith waddled back to his seat under the cherry tree and the officers went back to drilling their troops in the glare of the sun. Suddenly, a rider galloped up onto the lawn. It was the British spy, John Howe.

"Howe! What are you doing here? I thought

you'd be halfway across Massachusetts by now. Didn't you have letters?"

"Don't worry about the letters. They're all delivered. I have been halfway across Massachusetts. . . . But *you* . . . what are you doing in this deathtrap *drinking tea*?"

Colonel Smith turned red. The cup shook slightly in his hand.

"I've been to Salem," Howe went on, "and Danvers, and Gloucester, and Lynn, and every place you can name, almost. . . . Wherever I passed through, the story was the same. This land is up in arms! From every farmhouse, every market town, every seaport, the men are on the march. Those without guns carry swords, those without swords carry clubs or slings or bow and arrow. Those without horses go on foot. . . . Thousands!"

Howe was usually so calm and respectful. What had happened to make him shout like a madman? The news he brought was certainly frightening, but there was one rule Smith always observed—never to show fear.

"You forget one thing," he smiled. "When these *thousands*—as you call them—get here, they won't find a mere eight hundred. I'm expecting Lord Percy any minute now, with another thousand men."

"Maybe," Howe answered, "*maybe* Percy will be

here. But as sure as the sun moves westward, the Americans are moving toward this village. I swear they'll tear you to pieces if you don't clear out of Concord."

"Ridiculous!" Smith shrugged. "It's still early—" he pulled out his watch, "only 11:40. I won't have it said that a few bullets frightened the British Army out of Concord."

Howe turned away. "It's your funeral. Every minute will cost you men. But, of course, your vanity comes first." He faced Smith again. "Can you get me a fresh horse?"

"What for?"

"You don't think I'm fool enough to stay here and wait for my death? No, sir!"

"Are you heading back for Boston?"

"That's right."

"Well . . . when you meet Percy, tell him to hurry. And report to Gage that we had a little trouble at the Concord bridge—the North Bridge."

Howe was gone, but his words haunted the British commander. He lifted himself from the chair, and waddled over to his officers.

"Get the troops into formation, exactly as they were when we entered the village. In five minutes I'll give the signal to march. Remember, this has been a triumph for us. We entered the rebel stronghold without firing a shot. Controlled it for almost five hours. Destroyed every piece of public property we found, and lost fewer men than the rebels did, for all their boasts.

"When we march out, it must be with heads high. See that the weapons and uniforms are all in perfect order. And play "Yankee Doodle" so loud that the dead across the river will turn over in their sleep!"

They marched forth splendidly, but—behind their shutters—the women of Concord watched with mocking eyes. As soon as the last bayonet had disappeared, out rushed the women, the aged, and the children. Before anything else, they teamed up to save as much as possible of the powder that had been broken open. In this way they rescued half of the sixty barrels.

And while the women of Concord were laughing the King's best troops out of town, they wondered what their men had planned as a going away gift. For, surely, the royal troops would get a royal farewell.

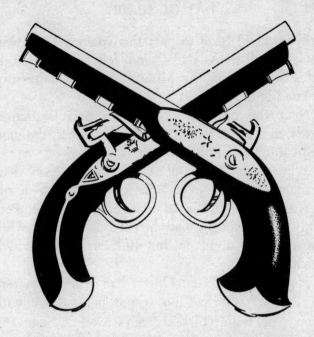

## DAY OF GLORY: *One P.M.*

*T*he Americans had not stood gaping at Smith's men. While the redcoats paraded back and forth in the center of the village, the patriots who'd been at the bridge, quietly prepared for the moment that was soon to come.

A few of the Acton men broke away. Theirs was the grim task of carrying Captain Davis and Abner Hosmer home. But the rest hurried across the great field toward the point where Bedford Road crossed Lexington Road. They knew the

British would have to pass this spot on their way back. With trees, rocks, and fences lining both sides of the road, the Minute Men could be sure of good hunting.

Near the crossing of Bedford and Lexington roads, at a place called Merriam's Corner, the men of Reading and Billerica waited.

When the news of Gage's expedition had reached the village of Billerica early that morning, there was a special kind of excitement. Perhaps other villages had listened in fear of what the redcoats might do, but Billerica said: "Watch what *we* do!"

A month ago, Tom Ditson had gone to market in Boston, and had not come home. Sick with worry, his wife had sent Tom's brother, Sam, and her own brother, John Blanchard, to search the road. But they'd found nothing.

The next day, rumors had reached Billerica. A young man of that village had been seized for "urging a British soldier to desert." Again Sam and John set out. This time, they galloped all the way to Boston and had no trouble finding Tom there.

Pushing through a crowd on one of the busy streets, they saw him. He'd been stripped, tarred and feathered, and tied to a cart. Soldiers of the 47th Regiment, commanded by Colonel Nesbitt, led the horrible procession to the tune of "Yankee Doodle."

When they brought Tom home that night, the whole village had rocked with anger. Some had cried out for revenge. But it was decided to wait for a better time.

And now the time had come. Among the first in Billerica to learn of Gage's expedition was Tom Ditson. His five children were still asleep when he left to join the Company on the Common. His brother and brother-in-law were already on the Green, waiting.

The Billerica Company marched up Bedford Road toward Concord, meeting their friends from Reading on the way. When they heard about the British defeat at North Bridge, they marched a little faster, fifed a little louder, and were almost at Merriam's Corner. Shh! Stop the fifing! There —on the hill—a hundred redcoats!

While they stood silently watching, the British marched down the hill with slow, steady step, without music. Just beyond, at a small bridge near the meeting of the roads, they suddenly faced about and fired a volley. The shots went wild; no one was hit.

Immediately, the Americans returned the fire. Two British soldiers fell dead. Peering ahead into the glare of the sun, Tom Ditson and his townsmen noticed a wood close to the road where the enemy would have to pass. They leaped over the walls and made for that wood, arriving just in time.

Across the road stood an orchard of apple trees. Suddenly, it seemed that every branch had turned into a musket, every blossom, a fistful of bullets. It was here the North Bridge men had taken a stand. They fired from trees that had once been seeds in their hands. The Billerica men fired from behind ancient maples and elms.

The enemy was now caught between two fires. Smith ordered out a flank guard on the left to chase the Americans from the woods. The flank became a better mark to be shot at.

The orchards and forests Smith had passed so quickly and gaily in the morning now seemed endless. Seeing that his flanks had been outflanked, Smith called them in. Now, the main body of his troops had no protection from the merciless trees.

At this point they were greeted by a new company—almost half of Woburn's four hundred men. All through the morning, couriers had come to their village with messages for Hancock and Adams.

Now, one hundred and eighty Woburn men fired at the enemy. They shot for themselves and they shot for Adams and Hancock.

Captain Parker rushed up from Lexington with the Harringtons, the Browns, the Munroes. . . .

They took their position, not behind trees, but in the fields of Lincoln—and poured a murderous fire into the enemy.

The fire was returned. Jedediah Munroe, wounded in the morning, died on this field. Solomon Brown saw his cousin Francis fall, with a bullet in the neck. The boy turned pale, loaded quickly, and fired. Then he fired again.

# DAY OF GLORY: *Two P.M.*

*W*here is Lord Percy?" The sweat running down his face, Pitcairn had galloped the length of the shattered line to ask Smith this question. "Where is he—with his thousand men? Did he hear the shooting and turn back like a sensible fellow?"

"He's on his way," Smith muttered. "If only we can get past these woods, and fight men, instead of trees . . ."

"What's he waiting for? Is Percy waiting for

us to be crushed first, and then make it his day of glory?" Pitcairn laughed bitterly.

"Stop talking about Percy, for God's sake! Let's find a way to keep our men together. Look at them!"

"What do you expect them to do—stand still and die? Remember, they've been on their feet since eight last night, while we've been on horseback. They're only men, and they hope to see the sun rise tomorrow."

The woods were thinning out. A sign said *Lexington.* There was a hill ahead. It might slow down the panic-stricken army.

Colonel Smith rattled off orders. "Now we'll show them what a real battle's like. They won't have trees to shield them here. Captains Parsons and Pole! Gather as many as you can, and take a position on that high bluff. You'll hold the rebels in check, while Pitcairn and I form the army on the hill. We'll see soon enough how brave those fellows are, out in the open."

It was a good plan, but by this time the Americans were moving like an April river. The rusty old guns had found their range. Attacking from all directions, the Yankees drove Parsons and Pole off the bluff, and surged forward, using every rock, every bush, as a shield.

Smith raged at his men. Yet the men slipped through his fingers. Scarcely half remained in the ranks. One of the officers, with drawn sword, rode back and forth, rallying the men, commanding them to load and fire.

All this while a party of Americans had been edging closer and closer. They were now in hiding nearby, behind a pile of rails.

Leading the Americans were the Acton men. From Luther Blanchard's wounded shoulder the fife hung silent. This was a time for gun music only.

The face of the young man was by now quite gray. James Hayward caught a look of pain in his eyes. He noticed a well at the foot of Fiske Hill, very close to where the British were regrouping for battle. "Sit down," he whispered, "I'll bring you water."

"No! You'll do no such thing!" Luther protested. "It's too close to them . . . I can wait—I'm not really thirsty."

But the young man, who'd sharpened his bayonet at daybreak, inched his way toward the well.

One of the redcoats had also seen the well and had rushed over to drink. At sight of the American, he drew his gun. "You are a dead man!"

"And so are you!" Hayward replied. They both fired. The redcoat died instantly. Hayward clutched his side of the wellhead, fighting for breath. His chest was shattered.

Now, suddenly, from behind the pile of rails,

the Americans poured a deadly volley into the British ranks. The officer who'd been rallying his men was unhorsed, and the frightened animal leaped over the wall.

Another officer clutched his bleeding leg and howled with pain. Could it be Smith? Who else on the hill was so fat? The other officers rushed to him. Of course, it was Smith!

Again the Yankees loaded, and fired. By this time, few red targets remained on Fiske Hill. It was April green again—except where the dead lay, forgotten.

But the Americans forgot nothing. Hayward, at the well, was given water to drink. Then, slowly, his fellow villagers carried the dying Acton lad into Lexington. At his side came Luther Blanchard, feverish from his own pain, but weeping for Hayward's. He put the fife to his parched lips, and as they moved down the road he played the tune his friend had asked for: "White Cockade."

"I killed the redcoat, didn't I?" Hayward murmured.

Luther nodded. "You shot him dead."

"Sorry . . . I couldn't bring you water . . ."

Far ahead, the guns sounded. "Our guns." They smiled.

It was true. By now, the British had neither the

ammunition nor the strength to make a stand. Breaking ranks, they ran, each looking out for himself alone.

"Do you think it might be wiser to surrender?" Pitcairn asked.

Smith was on his horse again, his bandaged leg cradled in the stirrup. "Surrender? To whom? To the trees? To the stone walls? Find me an officer among them, and I'll surrender! Not to a farmer with a flintlock from the French War!"

Smith was useless. Again, as they approached the Green of Lexington, Pitcairn found himself in command.

By ones, by twos, the army reached the tree-studded grassplot. They limped across it, panting for breath. Some had lost their guns, some, their wigs. The red woolen uniforms clung to their bodies, sloppy, tattered, drenched with sweat.

Parker and his men drove the King's troops before them. Shot after shot poured from their guns. This one for you, Isaac! And this for you, Caleb! For you, Jonas, and John, and Jonathan! For you, Robert, and Samuel, and Jedediah!

And this, for the dead of other villages, who woke at the word, Lexington! And this for you, Sam Adams, who promised the world we would show ourselves brave! And this for you, Gage, who refused to believe it.

Half a mile beyond, Percy waited. To frighten

the American guns into silence, he had placed the cannon on high ground. His army was formed into a hollow square.

Soon, Smith's force began stumbling into view. Gratefully they crawled inside the square that had been formed for their protection.

Percy had heard a great deal of shooting, and hoped for a full report—but one look at Smith's men was enough. Stretched out on the ground, unable to speak a word, they were their own report.

There would be time for talk later. Now wounds had to be patched up, and after a short breathing spell, guns had to be loaded for the homeward march.

Boston was still a long way off, and the sun was beginning to go down.

# DAY OF GLORY: *Three P.M.*

*F*rom the moment when Lexington's messenger had spoken, Joseph Warren's one thought had been to get to the scene of the fighting. Riding through Charlestown, he met Dr. Welch, a Son of Liberty. Dr. Welch was disturbed at the thought of Warren's riding into danger alone. Half the red-coat army would know him. In their present mood, they might easily shoot him down. At best they would take him prisoner.

The Charlestown patriot decided to ride with

his friend at least part of the way. Beyond Cambridge the two men came within sight of the rear of the British column, brilliant in the sun.

A few minutes after the army disappeared up the road, two laggard officers galloped up. "Where are the troops?" they asked excitedly.

"The troops?" Warren repeated. "What troops?"

The red-coated officers showed alarm. This was not good country to be lost in. After whispering together, they raced back toward Boston, and Warren laughed aloud.

"I'll be all right now," he said. "From this point it will be better if I go on alone."

Warren rode on toward Wetherby's tavern, at Menotomy, where the Committee of Safety would be meeting. He would stay an hour or two with them but no more. Committees were important. This particular committee was, in fact, the only real government in Massachusetts. Still, even the best committees had a habit of bogging down in talk, and this was one day when guns, not tongues, would make the final decisions.

The shutters and doors of the tavern were bolted. Warren rapped in the special way known only to Committee members. Silence . . . again he rapped, louder this time. Feet could be heard on the stairs, then a voice, behind the door. "Who is it?"

"It's Joseph Warren—let me in, please!"

The Committee was meeting upstairs, ready to escape again through the back window as they had in the night. They poured out the news. Percy had just marched past, without stopping. Lexington? Warren knew about that. Adams and Hancock? Safe, thanks to Warren's warning. They were in Woburn, when last heard from. They'd been moved from one house to another, and were now far from the scene of danger—though near enough to receive and send messages.

A few minutes later, the tremendous tidings from Concord arrived: North Bridge was in American hands!

"Smith will now clear out of Concord as soon as his pride allows it," Warren said, his spirit soaring.

More talk followed. Warren listened, waiting for a chance to speak. "Gentlemen!" he said, finally, "I'm not a military man. But one thing seems clear: our task is to prepare for the British return. Whatever might make Gage regret this day even more than he does already—must be done!"

"My thoughts are the same." General Heath nodded firmly. "If Percy decides to go home the way he came out, we can stop him at Cambridge's Great Bridge. I'd like to go down to Watertown and collect the militia there. We'll pull up the planks again—but this time we'll turn the bridge into a barricade, and give Percy a little fun."

The Committee agreed. Warren walked to the front door with his friend. He had something to ask, which the rest of the Committee had no need to hear. "When will you be done at Watertown, William?"

"What's it now—noon? Let's say I'll be done about two."

"Good. I'll meet you at the crossroads, and we'll go on together. By then, I'll know more of what's happening around Concord, and where we can find you an army."

An hour later, another courier burst into the Committee room. "Smith left Concord at noon. We met him at Merriam's Corner, then at Hardy Hill, then in the woods below Brook's tavern, then in the fields of Lincoln. We're driving his army like sheep down the Lexington road. Every tree, every stone wall, dooms them. Never in history has there been such a battle!"

For a moment, they were speechless. Warren, trembling, almost ready to weep for joy, quickly put on his coat.

"Who's in command of our forces?"

"In command?" The messenger laughed. "There is no command! The dead of Lexington Green are in command!"

They stopped Warren at the door. "Where are you going, Doctor?"

"Since you ask," he said softly, "I'm going with General Heath to Lexington."

"Impossible! We've appointed General Heath to command the companies in case of battle, and we're confident that he can handle the situation alone. Please sit down!"

Warren smiled gently, and turned the knob.

"We've had a very difficult time," they continued, "keeping Mr. Hancock away from Lexington today, sir, and we didn't expect to have to repeat our arguments with you!"

"Gentlemen," Joseph replied. "Mr. Hancock is needed in Philadelphia next month, not I. Believe me, nothing in this world could keep me from Lexington today."

In a moment he was on his horse and out of sight. Already he could hear, from the north, the sweet music of American muskets. At the crossroads he gave Heath the glorious news—America's forests were at war! Together they galloped off in the direction of Percy's cannon. The miles fell behind them. It was hardly three o'clock when the general and the doctor found their "army" in the woods around Lexington.

## DAY OF GLORY: *Four P.M.*

*W*ith a rear guard and two powerful flank
guards to protect Smith's men, Percy was marching triumphantly out of Lexington. How differently the regiments of Smith were behaving now! It
would be impossible for any onlooker to know
that these were the same men who, a little while
before, lay panting, panic-stricken on the ground.
Watching them now, Percy congratulated himself for having brought them back to life so
quickly. Not two hours ago, he'd gone to Smith

and said: "Look here, Colonel! I know your men have been through an unpleasant day. But we can't afford to let them behave this way."

Smith shrugged his shoulders. He had his own wound to think about. "You're in charge now. Do whatever you think is right."

Percy looked at his watch. "A quarter past two. They've had fifteen minutes to catch their breath. I intend to march them around the square a dozen times, with the bands playing, to get back some of their spirit. Then we'll head for Boston."

"Try it and see what happens!" Smith answered bitterly. "You think a fife and drum will get back their spirit? After the nightmare they've been through? Take a good look at them!

"I tell you at Fiske Hill they were close to mutiny! When I said the King pinned his faith on them, someone yelled: 'Let the King come here and hold the hill!' Don't forget, since you saw them last, these men have waded through marshes and trudged over dust. They've gone hungry and thirsty, felt the wind and the sun, dodged the bullets of an enemy they couldn't see. They've watched friends go down all around them!"

"What would *you* suggest?" Percy snapped. "Remember—*your* ammunition is gone altogether. My supply wagons disappeared unaccountably on the road so I haven't much more than you. Boston's a long way off, and we absolutely must get back before dusk!"

"What would I suggest?" Smith looked around at the neat village houses with their locked doors and tightly closed windows. "Of course, my men need rest, but what they want more, is food and drink and a little freedom. If you give them speeches now, if you make them march around, they'll blow up in your face. But if you give them half an hour of freedom and let them take over this village, they'll march home like new men."

Percy had agreed. He rode into the center of the square, and addressed Smith's men. "We leave in forty minutes. You may forage for food and drink, so long as you keep within range of our cannon. Any who are not back by three o'clock, will have to find their way home alone. Company dismissed!"

How they'd roared and jumped about and waved their hats in the air! Within seconds, the square became almost empty, as the redcoats staggered off in search of refreshment.

One of the protecting cannon was near William Munroe's tavern. Since last evening, Anna Munroe had hardly seen her husband. All through the cold, uncertain night, William Munroe had been leading his men back and forth in front of the Clark house.

At daybreak, it was William who formed the company on the Green. Later, he'd gone with the other Lexington men to meet the killers on their return from Concord.

If the men could do so much, Anna felt she could at least take her husband's place, here, in the tavern. John Raymond, just recovering from a long sickness which had prevented him from taking his place in the ranks of Minute Men, was in bed in an upper room. Except for the sick man, Anna Munroe was alone.

All at once there was a roar outside. Running to the window, Anna saw the redcoats cheering. Instantly, they poured out of the square, swarming toward the tavern and the houses nearby. Before she could move away from the window, at least fifty soldiers were through her door, with more on the way. They filled the front room.

No matter how quickly she poured the drinks, it was not quick enough. They dragged John Raymond out of bed, and made him wait on them. With drink, the King's soldiers grew brave again. They found it good sport to aim mugs at John Raymond's head. When they saw how pale and shaky he was, they asked insulting questions and mocked with laughter the trembling answers he tried to give. One of them shot a mug out of the sick man's hand.

Braver than ever, they pushed past Anna and

swaggered into the other rooms, smashing every lamp and window and mirror. Then they went to the second floor bent on more plunder. The stairs shook beneath their brave feet.

"Hurry, John!" Anna whispered. "There's no one at the door now. Slip out, for God's sake, or they'll finish you!"

"I won't leave you alone. They're out of their senses."

"Please, John, I'll be all right. They wouldn't dare molest a woman."

Trembling, he limped toward the door. But one of the redcoats had noticed. Bravely, he lifted the gun that had not spoken once on the road, and shot John Raymond dead.

With a scream, Anna rushed to the doorway and stooped to see if there was any life in her friend. Then, slowly, she looked up, and turned from face to face. "Monsters!" she cried, "you'll pay before this day is over!"

Bravely teams of redcoats broke down the doors of nearby buildings and swarmed inside. Jonathan Harrington and his father were both away with Captain Parker's company. His mother and young brothers were hiding in a safe place. The house was unprotected except for the locked doors.

The redcoats attacked the doors and windows. Once inside, they rifled the pantry shelves. Food that should have lasted a hundred meals disappeared in a few minutes. Then, leaving behind broken glasses and dishes, bones and pits and crumbs, they marched into other parts of the house.

By now, the courage of the British soldiers had reached its peak. The infant's cradle was smashed. Silverware, pottery from England disappeared into the pockets of the royal troops. Portraits were ripped from the walls, books were thrown out the window, a fine spinning wheel toppled over like a beaten enemy. How royally they fought—unafraid of the Harringtons' empty house! When there was nothing more to smash or steal, they set fire to the house and swarmed out.

Nearby were the house and shop of Lydia Mulliken. Here, too, the door had to be broken down. Bravely, the redcoats burst past the little padlock as though it were the gates of a great city. From room to room they wheeled, taking what they could carry, destroying the rest, before setting house and shop afire.

In the shadow of the other cannon across the square, soldiers proved their courage. Joshua Bond, the saddle and harness maker, was loyal to the King. As a reward for his loyalty they left to him a heap of ashes.

That morning, looking out the window, the saddlemaker had laughed to see his neighbor, Nat Farmer, running toward the Green with his gun

—leaving behind six young children and his wife.

An hour later, looking out again, Joshua Bond had seen Nathaniel stumble home—the bone of his right arm crushed by a bullet.

"Now, if I'd gone with him," he had murmured, "that might've been the end of saddle-making for me." Yet the fool had torn himself away from his wife's arms at noon, and gone off again, saying, "It doesn't hurt much. This time I want to meet them face to face." Now, Joshua saw his own house go up in flames. Nothing remained— no trace of his fine saddles and harnesses.

From house to house the King's men moved, always under protection of Percy's cannon. Watching from the woods, young Jonathan Loring started to run toward his father's burning house. Solomon Brown and Elijah Sanderson grabbed him and pulled him back. "You can't stop them. They'll only kill you." Jonathan turned away, so as not to see the charred roof. "The day's not over yet, we'll pay them back," Solomon told him.

The Yankee walls, the Yankee roofs sang such a delightful tune as they crumbled and crashed. Some redcoats were deaf to the signaling fifes.

"The fifes!" someone finally yelled. "It must be three o'clock!"

"So soon! What a shame to leave this sport half finished! So many buildings, with hardly a scratch on them!"

"Come on back; you heard Percy. He'll leave us behind!"

The wilder ones had to be dragged away. "Just that barn! That fence!" Fire seemed to have become a part of them.

No longer tired, they formed into columns at Percy's command. If only the breeze were stronger, so the fire would spread to the woods! To the hateful trees . . .

Lord Percy did not approve of the burning and plundering, but now was not the time to scold. The soldiers were alert and brave again. He could ask for nothing more. Leaving behind a mile of ashes, the King's troops marched out of Lexington.

The Yankees had disappeared into thin air. They'd evidently had enough for one day. They knew what was best for them.

Percy smiled. "I guess the rebels have gone home to boast. Four o'clock! At this rate we should be in Boston for an early supper."

## DAY OF GLORY: *Five P.M.*

*F*or two miles Percy had no trouble. Then he heard shots at the rear. "A few die-hards!" he thought. "Nothing to be concerned about."

Soon, the British column descended from the high grounds onto the plain of Menotomy. At the foot of the rocks, the redcoats were suddenly hit by a savage volley. "Wrong, Percy!" the Yankee guns seemed to cry. "We've not gone home yet!"

True, some from the northern villages were no longer in the fight. At Lexington, catching sight

of Percy's reinforcements, these farmers felt there
was nothing further to be gained. They'd done
enough for one day. An even stronger argument
against staying was the deadly thunder of the
two fieldpieces.

Heath and Warren had reached Lexington while
trees were still trembling from a cannonade.
"Look!" the doctor pointed. "Aren't those some of
our men walking away?"

General Heath peered through the woods. Sure
enough, at least a dozen Americans, with muskets
slung over their shoulders, could be seen slowly
disappearing. Nearby, groups of Minute Men
seemed to be arguing. As the two leaders galloped up, they heard someone exclaim: "Well,
*I'm* going. I can't see any sense in this."

Warren jumped off his horse and tied it to
a tree. Before the farmer who'd just spoken could
turn away, the doctor's arm was on his shoulder.
"What's happening?" he asked.

The group turned in amazement. "Dr. Warren!
and General Heath!" The news of their arrival
spread; from behind a hundred trees others ran
up.

"What's happening?" Warren repeated. It was
explained that some of the men had left and
others were arguing that they should all disband.

"Disband?" the doctor cried. "With Percy

trapped among our woods, and fifteen miles to go?"

"I can't force you to keep fighting," said Heath. "No matter what happens from now on, America will be grateful for what you've already done. I know you must be tired and hungry. Some of you have lost sons, brothers, friends. A few are wounded, I see.

"If the reason for disbanding," he went on, "is that you haven't the strength to continue, I release you. But if it's because you think we haven't a chance against such a large number, against cannon, then I must say you're dead wrong.

"From stone walls and buildings, what difference will it make to us how many redcoats pass on the road? They'll have their hands full keeping Smith's eight hundred on the move, after what you did to them.

"And as for the cannon—if you don't know—" Warren added, with a smile, "the old men of Menotomy captured Percy's supply wagon. He has hardly any ammunition to fall back on. Every time he fires he'll be nearer to having no powder and shot at all."

There was no more talk of disbanding. The men moved through the woods, choosing spots near the road from which to shoot. Pushing ahead, Heath led the main body of his little army to the foot of the rocks at Menotomy, where they took up positions and waited.

Warren rushed from group to group, signaling the approach of the redcoats, pointing out the officers to be aimed at.

"Fire!" he cried, again and again. "Down!" he barked, when he saw the British aiming at his men. But he himself had no time to duck bullets. There was always another group to be reached.

Once in a while someone would call out, "Take care, Doctor! They see you. Get behind that tree!" But there was no time.

A strong wind started up, and blew the smoke of the British guns back into their own eyes. Those few who had the courage to fire back at the enemy had little luck. By the time they loaded and took aim, there was no one behind the wall to shoot at. Only Warren was everywhere— an easy mark.

A musketball whizzed by Warren's head. "Are you all right, Joseph?" Heath cried.

"Fine," the doctor smiled.

"Well," said the general, looking him over with a frown, "you're a very lucky fellow. That ball just struck the pin out of the hair of your earlock. Being in command here, Joseph, I order you to keep your head on! We can't afford to lose it."

But Warren had to hurry away. A lad was bleeding.

Percy thought of stopping and making a stand. But the sun was going down too quickly, and Boston was still far away. Besides, he was down to thirty-six rounds of ammunition. So he ordered his troops to move faster.

A little farther on, the rebel ranks swelled as fresh men came in. The companies of Roxbury, Dorchester and Brookline had wisely waited for this moment. Concord had been too far for them to reach in time. They knew Percy would be coming back this way soon enough, and made good use of the hours by gathering ammunition. They made Menotomy a different place from what it had appeared to be at noon. Every house was suddenly crowded with guns.

All at once, Percy turned on the rebels with a killing cannonade. But Warren roared at the top of his lungs: "It won't work this time, Percy!" and ran out into the road, shooting back at the cannoneers.

The British flank guard was strong, but not strong enough to cope with such fighters, who kept on the move, loading their pieces at one place, and discharging them at another. Setting houses afire was so much easier!

Behind Cooper's tavern, eighty-one-year-old Samuel Whittemore made his stand. He had been among those who captured the supply wagons which Percy needed so badly. Afterwards, when others fled to the hills, Whittemore's children urged the old man to come with them. But he sat knocking his flint and said he would not go. "I must get a shot at the redcoats when they come back. If I can only be the instrument of killing one of my country's enemies, I shall die in peace."

Now he crouched behind a stone wall. When five redcoats approached, he discharged the gun. A soldier fell dead. Then, with a pistol, he killed another. While raising his second pistol, a ball struck his face and shot away part of his cheekbone. The old man fell, and the three remaining soldiers jumped over the wall, striking him with their bayonets again and again.

His hat and clothes had been pierced through in many places. His head was covered with blood. "We've killed the old rebel," they said.

But Samuel Whittemore's heart was beating miraculously—his heart would surprise them, as the drums of his country had surprised them.

# DAY OF GLORY: *Six P.M.*

*C*olonel Barnard left his men and galloped over to Lord Percy. "Which road do we take from Menotomy?"

This question was exactly what Percy had been asking himself for the past half hour. He was quite sure by now which way he would have to go. Of course, Governor Gage had planned things differently. "You'll march back the way you came —past Cambridge and Roxbury, and in through the town gate—slowly, proudly, with bayonets fixed

and with bands playing so loud, that the spoons
will shake on every table!"

The triumphant return was to have taken place
at four o'clock, under a bright sun. How could
the governor imagine things would turn out *this*
way? How could he know the sun would be setting?

No, Your Excellency, Percy decided, I'll have
no more business today with the Great Bridge.
If the rebels were fool enough to leave the planks
nearby this morning, they won't make the same
mistake now. A fine thing it would be: trapped
at the river, with the sun gone, the powder gone,
and enemy trees all around us!

"No, Your Excellency," he mumbled, while the
bullets flew by, "even if we could get across the
river, I'll not be seen in Roxbury again: with
every empty house turning into a barricade and
that saucy little fellow singing his saucy little ballad again.

"The road to Charlestown won't be easy, but
it's shorter, and the country's more open. Once
we get near the ships, I'll make a stand. They
won't dare challenge me then. But first . . . to
get past this village, to put behind me these
death-spitting houses and walls!"

Beyond the next winding of the road Percy
could see the top of a hill. Through his spyglasses

he made out a large group of Americans, busily preparing to greet him.

"Miller! Take fifty good men out of the line and lead them around to the back of that hill. There's a number of rebels waiting to fire at us. Get in back of them."

The walled enclosure stood on the side of the hill facing the road. Part of the Americans had taken up positions in the open, behind trees; others had gone inside the enclosure, and piled shingles, which were lying there, to make their breastwork stronger.

From the way they went about their preparations, it was clear that these hundred men felt very confident. When Percy's army came into view, they took aim. As they fired, Miller's men closed in, from the rear.

Caught between two fires, the Americans turned and fled. Some ran toward a nearby house, whose owner had come out to help them. The owner, a lame man, limped in behind them, and locked the door.

Before they had time to take cover, the doors and windows were broken through. A few of the men managed to get down the cellar stairs. They shot at every redcoat who tried to come down after them. The others, including the man of the house, were killed.

As though to make up for the comrades who were dead, the surviving Americans took a position behind a wall, from which they sent a merciless fire into the British lines.

Back on the road, Lieutenant Miller sought out Percy. "Is something wrong?" he asked.

"Is something wrong?" Percy roared. "No, nothing's wrong. Everything's going according to plan—Samuel Adams' plan! You see, I'm on a different horse. Mine was shot by mistake. The bullets were meant for me! Barnard over there, poor chap, they made no mistake with him. How'd it go on that hill?"

Miller told him how the Americans had been overwhelmed.

"Good! Very good!" Percy's eyes brightened. "How many prisoners did you take?"

"Four surrendered, sir, but I couldn't stop my men from killing them."

"Idiots! Must it be spelled out for you why I need prisoners? How else can we hope to exchange our own captured men? How else can I get information? At least one, Lieutenant; you could've saved *one!*"

"I tried to, sir, believe me, I tried. But the men simply wouldn't listen. After all, they've stood a lot from these bumpkins."

"Where were they from—these newcomers?" Percy asked. "I hope you found that out."

"Danvers, sir. One of them yelled it before he saw us. He yelled it right down at your heads, while he loaded and took aim. 'Thirsty, are you?' he yelled. 'Well, here's a toast from Danvers . . . taste it!' "

Percy turned around in disbelief. "Did you say *Danvers?*"

"That's right. And now that I think of it, I remember something else he said just before I drove my bayonet through his back. 'If you like the way it tastes when a hundred of us pour it, just wait for the seven hundred Essex men that are coming in an hour or so!' "

Miller looked away, and mumbled to himself: "I plunged the bayonet through his back, as he fired. Then he turned round a little to see who had killed him. He looked young, eighteen, or nineteen at most."

"Danvers! A hundred from Danvers!" Percy couldn't get it out of his head. "Danvers is sixteen miles from here. Sixteen miles on foot in four hours! How could they do it, unless they ran half the way? Imagine! *Running half the way, so as not to miss us! How they must hate us!*"

He looked at his watch: six o'clock. Then at the sky. Hardly an hour of suntime left. Shadows of trees already gripped the road. If only he could find a dependable messenger to send ahead. But who, in a red coat, would dare to move through these roads alone?

Who could tell Gage what must be told? That two hundred men had been lost; that Roxbury was out of the question. That the army was heading for Bunker Hill but might never get there. That reinforcements must be sent and every ship in the fleet must be drawn up at the Charlestown shore.

Other things, too, must be told to Gage. It must be made known, tomorrow, if not tonight, that His Excellency had been wrong, dead wrong, about these men who called themselves "Sons of Liberty." They were far from a clumsy mob. There were men among them who knew very well what they were about. How could His Excellency have forgotten how these men had fought against the Indians and French?

"Gage may not think so, nor the Ministers in London—but these men have declared war, and are likely to win. I must get a messenger through!" he muttered.

But Gage knew. He needed no messengers. Plenty of spies were in the streets and taverns of Boston, wherever people were whispering and smiling together.

When John Howe burst in, the governor stopped him before he could gasp out his first word. "Are *you* also going to tell me the great news about Concord?"

Howe was hurt. Since last night he hadn't stopped riding.

"It was you, wasn't it," Gage continued, "who advised me against trying Worcester? 'Concord's safer,' you told me, 'and the supplies collected there are worth a night's march.' Well, tell me now. Was it safe at Concord? Was it worth while?"

John Howe was no hypocrite, like some of the other Tories. Now, as always, he spoke his mind. "Worcester would've been ten times worse. I was there when the bells rang for Lexington. If Smith had gone to Worcester, you'd not see a single man of the eight hundred ever again!"

Gage tried not to pace back and forth, tried not to wring his hands. "What other news?"

"Colonel Smith was still in Concord when I left before noon—waiting for Percy. And where do you think I found Lord Percy? In Lexington, waiting for Smith!"

Gage rose, trembling with anger. "I asked for news, sir. All Boston has known this past half hour that Smith left Concord at noon and was ripped apart on Lexington road."

Howe turned pale. "I was afraid of that."

Smashing his fist against the table, the governor roared, "Again and again they've let me down, one after the other!"

Howe looked down. Among the officers, most of the blame was laid at Gage's own doorstep. He'd been too gentle with the rebels, they said. He should've arrested Sam Adams long before. The spy got up to go. "Is that all, sir?"

The governor had gone to the window and stood looking down, as if no one else were in the room. "You know where to find me," said Howe.

Alone now, Gage stood at his window, watching the shadows grow long and deep, learning— through the ripples of laughter on Boston's streets —of his disaster. He needed no messenger to tell him which way Percy would come. Of course it must be Charlestown. Of course the battleships must be drawn up and reinforcements ferried over.

But while he made all the proper arrangements, one thought kept drumming in his mind: *How shall I put it all down on paper? What words can I find for the eyes of my King?*

# DAY OF GLORY: *Seven P.M.*

*L*ook!" Dolly had stuck her head out of the carriage window, and was admiring the setting sun. "In a few minutes it'll be gone."

The others took turns looking out; first Aunt Lydia, then Hancock, finally, Adams. It was certainly a sight to remember. About to vanish, the sun seemed to have taken into itself all the blood of the day. Like a bowl of blood it hung on the horizon.

Her companions were grateful to Dolly for breaking the silence. Since they'd left Billerica, hardly a word had passed between them. Partly, it was the gentle rhythm of the carriage that had put their tongues to sleep. But, mostly, it was the events of this day, which they had to study over and over, remembering sights and sounds that could not lightly be turned into words.

Both women were haunted by what they'd witnessed at daybreak, from the Clark house windows. They'd seen it from beginning to end: the farmers of Lexington parading their Green; the invaders firing; the farmers dispersing—those who still lived. Then, the British savagely cheering!

They would never forget the look on the faces of the two wounded men, carried into the Clark house. Nor the look on Parson Clark's face when he came home from his prayer for the dead on the Green!

Hancock and Adams also had scenes to remember, especially one moment at dawn. There'd been a long, heavy silence after they'd stopped the carriage in the Woburn woods. Then, suddenly, in the distance, a song of guns. At the same instant, the first sunrays had burst across the world.

"Oh, what a glorious morning for America!" Adams had cried out. Then, they'd climbed back into the carriage and hurried on: fugitives from the soldiers of the King. Now, in triumph, the carriage was rolling back along the same road, while those who'd been sent to seize them were fugitives.

The sun was disappearing. How it had changed on this one journey from east to west! At dawn, so glittering yellow; at dusk, dull red, drenched in blood.

They turned from the sunset, back to silence and thought. Hancock was impatient to be in Lexington again; thirty-six hours without sleep . . . twenty-four hours since the last real food. The salmon Dolly had brought—Mrs. Clark's promised salmon—had gone uneaten. The British had been too close. They had had to flee, taking the ladies with them, before they could taste it.

First of all, Hancock felt he must get out of his clothes. They were heavy with sweat, spattered with mud, and a little torn. Imagine, a Hancock jumping over ditches, huddling in closets, hiding in swamps in silk hose and velvet coat!

Adams was also eager to be back. Letters must be written, letters that Revere would carry to leaders in other colonies. Ways must be found of getting a full report to London before the lies of Gage could get there. A call to arms must be issued to the men of Massachusetts. And a warning must somehow reach Betsey, that she and the children had better clear out of Boston at once.

Night was coming on. The air grew chilly. The carriage bumped along the road. That house with the light in the window was within the boundaries of Lexington! Another light, and another, and then, the stark, charred frame, where a house had been. The burned house was no surprise. The news of the burning had reached Adams at Billerica.

The horses stopped. Ah! here were Jonas and Lucy Clark and the children waiting to help them down. Adams took a deep breath. The air smelled of charred homes, of burnt cradles. They walked into the house.

"There's a turkey waiting to be eaten," Lucy Clark announced, as though nothing extraordinary had occurred. "And then you two will go straight to bed!"

Adams shook his head. "Not for a while, Madam. Mr. Hancock and I will be wanting to meet with some of the villagers first. We could not sleep otherwise."

All through the meal, visitors came in. Word had spread that the two leaders were back in Lexington. The villagers had to see them, for it was their hope to hear from Adams' lips the full meaning of this day.

Instead, it was *he* who asked questions. Had they lost anyone near and dear? Had their property been plundered by the enemy? Had they seen or heard anything which should be made known?

Most of the men were still away, with Warren and Heath. But news was coming back from
the road. Adams bent forward, the fork raised in
his hand. Yes—great news—of British disaster; of
a hundred Danvers men who had run sixteen
miles to reach the road in time; of Brookline,
Milton, Dorchester, Roxbury, joining the battle;
and, over and over, of Joseph Warren.

Whatever the news, somehow, one name had to
be spoken: Joseph Warren. It was as though he'd
multiplied himself and was now ten men, each
with miraculous power.

Adams beamed. "It seems we've lost a doctor
and gained a general. Don't you agree, John," he
turned to Hancock, "that Warren should issue the
call to arms?"

The frown on Hancock's face surprised him.
Adams had expected to find a proud smile match-
ing his own.

The wealthy merchant murmured, "Of course!
Who else but Warren?"

Adams understood. Hancock wanted to issue the
call to arms—just as he'd wanted to deliver the
Massacre Day speech last month; just as he'd
wanted to be seen on the field of battle all last
night and all this day.

Had the two leaders been alone, Adams might
have said something about envy and vanity. He
let the words wait for a better moment. Perhaps

they would never be spoken. In time of war, quarrels must be put aside. John Hancock had much to offer America: bravery, money, and a good name. *Be patient with him,* Adams told himself for the hundredth time. *Some change more slowly than others.*

After supper, on the way to see what was left of the Loring house, Adams said, softly, "You know, John, we two shall have big enough battles in a few weeks. To speak of independence in Philadelphia will be much like firing a cannon."

For a moment, Hancock was silent. Then he murmured, "I must confess that I envy Joseph Warren tonight. To be on that road, dodging bullets, tearing Percy apart—I'd have given half my fortune!"

At that instant, on Charlestown Common, it was of Joseph Warren that a hundred fighters spoke. "Did you notice him at the foot of the rocks?" "Did you see him at Watson's Corner?" "The way he spoke—man to man—no airs about him!" "It was Dr. Warren sent Revere to warn us!"

They were waiting, this little army, for Heath, Warren and some of the Company commanders to finish the council of war they were holding at the foot of Prospect Hill.

Half an hour before, Percy had finally escaped them. He had managed to drag his shattered col-

umn through Charlestown Neck and onto Bunker
Hill.

Heath had ordered the halt. Battleships stood
offshore at the Neck and reinforcements would
easily get across from Boston. An open battle was
exactly what Gage wanted.

So the farmers waited on the Common, and
watched Gage's bloody sun go down. They realized suddenly, that they were very tired and hungry. Still, they hoped General Heath would not
tell them to go home. It felt good standing shoulder to shoulder, hundreds who'd never seen one
another before this day, but who were now forever one.

The council broke up. The officers walked toward them. As Warren passed, a cheer broke the
stillness.

One of the fifers began to play a melody which
Warren recognized as "British Grenadier." A year
ago, he'd scribbled down some new stanzas to the
old tune, and Sam Adams had insisted it be
printed in the newspaper.

Were his ears playing tricks? It seemed some
of the men were taking up the melody, and singing the words he'd written! Yes—there was no
question of it.

He motioned for them to stop, so that General
Heath could make his announcement, but for the
first time that day they refused to take Joseph

Warren's orders. By the time they'd come to the fourth stanza, half the men on the Common were shouting the song—

> *Lift up your hearts, my heroes, and swear,*
> *    with proud disdain,*
> *The wretch that would ensnare you shall*
> *    spread his net in vain;*
> *Should Europe empty all her force, we'd*
> *    meet them in array,*
> *And shout huzza! huzza! huzza! for brave*
> *    America!*

Heath was puzzled by the strange behavior, until one of the officers whispered into his ear that this was Warren's song the men were singing. The general nodded, and put his arm around his friend's shoulder.

Heath waited for the echo of the song to be carried away by the strong wind, away to the ears of the British army, to Boston—and to London. Then he stepped forward and said, "Men— the army will camp in Cambridge overnight. Those who wish to return home may do so."

The three Lexington lads, Solomon Brown, Jonathan Loring, and Elijah Sanderson, looked at one another. He had called them an *army!* Return home? Who could think of such a thing now?

The fifers and drummers marched ahead, and

the little army followed, singing. As they moved off the Common and headed for Cambridge, the sentries Percy had posted at Charlestown Neck listened without smiling:

*Torn from a world of tyrants, beneath this western sky*
*We formed a new dominion, a land of liberty:*
*The world shall own we're freemen here, and such will ever be.*
*Huzza! huzza! huzza! huzza! for love and liberty!*